DISCARD

378.1
GRI

000010001254499

Direct Hits Toughest Vocabulary of the SAT: Volume 2

2011 Edition

By Larry Krieger

Edited by Ted Griffith

D0456791

This copy belongs to:

_____

Copyright © 2011 by Direct Hits Publishing

All Rights Reserved. No part of this book may be reproduced in any form or by any electronic or mechanical means, including information storage and retrieval systems, without permission in writing from the publisher, except by a reviewer who may quote brief passages in a review.

For more information, please contact us by mail:

Direct Hits Publishing
2639 Arden Rd., Atlanta GA 30327
Ted@DirectHitsPublishing.com

Or visit our website:
www.DirectHitsPublishing.com

Third Edition: August 2010

ISBN 10:   0-9818184-6-3

ISBN 13:   978-0-9818184-6-7

Edited by Ted Griffith

Cover Design by Carlo da Silva

Interior Design by Katherine Goodman

SAT is a registered trademark of Educational Testing Service (ETS). This publication is not endorsed or approved by ETS.

FAIR USE NOTICE: This publication contains copyrighted material the use of which has not always been specifically authorized by the copyright owner. We are making such material available in limited form in our endeavor to educate students on advanced vocabulary through the use of vivid illustrations to enable pursuit of higher academic goals and opportunities. We believe this constitutes a 'fair use' of any such copyrighted material as provided for in section 107 of the US Copyright Law. If you wish to use copyrighted material from this publication for purposes of your own that go beyond 'fair use', you must obtain permission from the copyright owner.

We would like to acknowledge and give credit to the following for use of their work and / or name, that any copyrights on such materials remain their respective property and that this publication is not endorsed or approved by: 19 Entertainment, 50 Cent, ABC Studios, Amblin Entertainment, American Idol Productions, Amy Winehouse, Anthony Kiedis, Anvil Films, Apple Inc., Bad Robot, Battlefield Productions LLC, Big Beach Productions, Blue Wolf, Capella International, CBS Television, Coach Carter, Cher, Colombia Pictures, CW Television Network, Disney/Pixar, DreamWorks Pictures, DreamWorks SKG, Dylan Sellers Productions, Eric's Boy, Expired, F Scott Fitzgerald, Fireworks Pictures, Four by Two, Fox, GH Three, The Grammies, Harper Lee, HBO, Helen Hunt Jackson, Hurston, J.K. Rowling, Lawrence Bender Productions, Lions Gate Films, Lucas Film, Martin Luther King, Marvel Studios, Metro Goldwyn Mayer, Michael Jackson, MTV, MTV films, 'N Sync, NCAA, New Line Cinema, New Orleans Times-Picayune, NFL, Nobel Prize, The Oscars, Paramount Pictures, Rachel Carson, Revolution Studios, Shakespeare, Tony Dungy, Touchstone Pictures, Tri-Star Pictures, Twentieth Century Fox Film Corporation, Universal Pictures, Walt Disney Pictures, Warner Brothers Pictures, Warner Brothers Television.

Acknowledgements

This book would not have been possible without the help of great students, dedicated friends and a tireless Product Manager. I would like to thank the following students for their valuable suggestions: Kate Armstrong, Jacob Byrne, Jill Reid, Lindsey Brenner, Misha Milijanic, Britney Frankel, Charlie Griffith, and Joey Holland. Special thanks to Lauren Treene, Evan Hewel, Holland McTyeire, and Alex Washington for their ability to help me connect vivid movie scenes with difficult SAT words.

I would also like to thank Jan Altman for her original research compiling lists of key SAT words. As always, Jane Armstrong's unfailing enthusiasm inspired our creative energies. Additionally, thank you to Jane Saral for careful proofreading and clarification of all grammar questions. Extra special thanks to Claire Griffith for her encouragement and creative ideas, and to Luther Griffith for his keen insights and impeccable judgment.

This book would not have been possible without a dedicated Product Manager. Ted Griffith has been everything an author could ask for - resourceful, innovative, and meticulous.

And finally, I am deeply grateful for the "close reads," patience, and love of my wife, Susan.

Table of Contents

Introduction

Most students believe that learning new words is a tedious chore that involves memorizing long lists of "big" but useless vocabulary words. Like Volume 1, this book is designed to provide you with a new and different approach to learning challenging vocabulary.

Volume 2 features 200 words that have all appeared on recent SATs. Each of these words is illustrated with an ECLECTIC (varied) mix of examples taken from pop culture, historic events, and contemporary issues. For example, you'll discover that the writers of *Gossip Girl* and Taylor Swift share a PENCHANT (liking) for using literary ALLUSIONS (references), while Queen Elizabeth I and Rick "The Big Boss" Ross share a passion for OSTENTATIOUS (showy) jewelry. You'll also learn about the ENTREPRENEUR (person who organizes and manages a business) who founded Facebook and the IDIOSYNCRASIES (distinctive traits) of the cast of *Jersey Shore*.

Volume 2 is designed to tackle challenging words that often appear in Level 4 and Level 5 questions. We begin with 15 literary terms and 45 words taken from science and the social sciences. These 60 academic words all appear in your textbooks and on the SAT.

Our next chapter defines and illustrates 20 words that look familiar but have multiple meanings. These everyday words such as FLAG, CHECK, and COIN have surprising secondary meanings that can trick unsuspecting students.

Introduction

The final two chapters focus upon the 120 toughest words on the SAT. Each of these words has appeared as an answer or answer choice to a Level 5 question. Learning these words is guaranteed to raise your Critical Reading score.

I hope you enjoy learning the vocabulary words in Volume 2. I also want you to test your ability to use these words. Each SAT includes 48 critical reading questions and 19 sentence completion questions. Chapter 6 concludes with a set of 5 critical reading questions. You'll find a set of 10 sentence completion questions at the end of Chapters 7-10. In addition, Volume 2 concludes with a Final Review that contains 10 more sentence completion questions and 5 more critical reading questions. Taken together, the 60 questions in this volume will give you an opportunity to test your vocabulary on SAT questions.

So what are you waiting for? Taylor Swift, Queen Elizabeth I, Rick Ross, The "Situation," and a host of superheroes, celebrities, and historic figures are all waiting and eager to help you AUGMENT (increase) your vocabulary and raise your Critical Reading scores.

About Larry Krieger

Larry Krieger is one of the foremost SAT experts in the country. His renowned teaching methods and SAT prep courses are praised for both their inventive, engaging approaches and their results. Students under Krieger's guidance improve their SAT scores by an average of 200 points.

Formerly a social studies supervisor and AP Art History teacher at New Jersey's SAT powerhouse Montgomery Township High School near Princeton, Krieger led the school to a Number 1 ranking in the state and nation for a comprehensive public high school. In 2004, Montgomery students achieved a record national average score of 629 on the Critical Reading section of the SAT.

Beginning in 2005, the College Board recognized Krieger's AP Art History course as the "strongest in the world" for three straight years. With an open enrollment, 60 percent of the senior class took the course and 100 percent made grades of 3 or higher, including some special education students.

Krieger is the co-author of several US History, World History, and AP Art History texts used throughout the country. He earned a BA in history and an MAT from University of North Carolina at Chapel Hill and an MA in sociology from Wake Forest.

Though Krieger admits to being completely unprepared for his first SAT in high school, he regularly takes the SAT to keep up with changes on the new test.

Chapter 6

KEY LITERARY TERMS: 201–215

Many students believe that literary terms such as SYNOPSIS, ANECDOTE, and ALLUSION are limited to language arts classes and tests. Nothing could be further from the truth. We often tell our friends summaries of favorite television shows, describe humorous incidents, and make brief references to people and events. Literary terms are part of our everyday life. SAT test writers are also aware of the importance of literary terms. As a result, most exams include questions designed to determine if you can recognize IRONY, METAPHORICAL language, and literary CARICATURES. This chapter defines and illustrates 15 frequently tested literary terms. As you study each term in this chapter, try to think of additional examples from your reading and daily life.

201. SYNOPSIS:

A brief summary of the major points of a thesis, theory, story or literary work; an abstract; a PRÉCIS

Has anyone ever asked you to summarize a movie, television show, or a YouTube clip? If you did, you provided them with a SYNOPSIS or brief summary. Here is a SYNOPSIS of the movie *The Hangover*: Three groomsmen inexplicably lose their soon-to-be married buddy during a wild bachelor party and must try to find him by following strange clues that include a tiger, a missing tooth, and a six-month-old baby.

202. SIMILE:

A figure of speech, often introduced by 'like' or 'as', which compares two unlike things

METAPHOR:

A figure of speech in which a comparison is made between two unrelated objects

Here are three examples of SIMILES:

- Death lies on her, like an untimely frost.
  ~ William Shakespeare

- The apple-green car with the white vinyl roof and Florida plates turned into the street like a greased cobra.
  ~ Gloria Naylor

- You know the type, loud as a motor bike
  But wouldn't bust a grape in a fruit fight.
  ~ Jay-Z

Here are three examples of METAPHORS:

- In the movie *High School Musical 2*, Taylor compares Sharpay to an octopus when she warns Gabriella, "that girl's got more moves than an octopus in a wrestling match."

- In the movie *The Dark Knight*, the Joker compares himself to a dog and a wrench when he tells Batman, "You know what I am? I'm a dog chasing cars. I wouldn't know what to do if I caught one. I just 'do' things. I'm a wrench in the gears."

- In the novel *The Falling Woman*, archaeologist Elizabeth Butler compares herself to a loner when she explains, "In academic circles, I linger on the fringes where the warmth of the fire never reaches, an irreverent outsider, a loner who prefers fieldwork to the university, and general readership to academic journals."

◎ Tip for a Direct Hit

SAT test writers sometimes use "figurative language" and "metaphorical language" as answers. Don't let these phrases confuse you. If the passage contains either a SIMILE or a METAPHOR it is an example of either figurative or metaphorical language. For example, in *The Bonesetter* by Amy Tan, LuLing instructs her daughter to "draw the stroke with grace, like a bird landing on a branch." Since the phrase uses a SIMILE, it is also notable for its use of metaphorical language.

203. PERSONIFICATION:

A figure of speech in which an inanimate object is given human qualities or abilities

PERSONIFICATION is used in essays, poems, and stories to convey an attitude or illustrate an idea. It is also used in advertisements to promote a product. For example, Bib, the Michelin Man, PERSONIFIES trust, caring, and quality. Advertising slogans rely on PERSONIFICATION too. For example, Goldfish snack crackers are "the snack that smiles back."

204. IRONY:

A form of speech in which what we say or write conveys the opposite of its literal meaning

IRONY involves the perception that things are not what they are said to be or what they seem.

Here are some examples of IRONY:

- In *Star Wars*, Han Solo tells Jabba the Hutt, "Jabba, you're a wonderful human being." Jabba is, in fact, neither wonderful nor a human being!

- In Shakespeare's *Julius Caesar*, Marc Antony gives a famous IRONIC speech in which he repeats "And Brutus is an honorable man," when Brutus has just killed Julius Caesar and is not honorable at all!

- In Sophocles' *Oedipus Rex* it is IRONIC that Oedipus thinks he is the detective in finding out who killed his predecessor, when he is actually, IRONICALLY, the murderer.

205. SATIRE, LAMPOON, PARODY:

A work that ridicules human vices and follies; comic criticism. Note that LAMPOON and PARODY are often used as verbs meaning to ridicule.

What do the ancient Greek playwright Aristophanes and the modern comedian Tina Fey have in common? Both mastered the art of using SATIRE to mock public figures. In his play *The Clouds*, Aristophanes LAMPOONS Socrates as an ABSTRUSE (very abstract, hard to understand) philosopher who operates a "Thinking Shop." Perched in a basket suspended from the ceiling, Socrates teaches his students how to prove anything, even if it is false.

Although it is a long way from Socrates' "Thinking Shop" to Tina Fey's *Saturday Night Live* skits, the principle of using SATIRE to mock public figures remains the same. In a series of now iconic PARODIES, Fey SATIRIZED Sarah Palin by aiming comic barbs at the Republican vice-presidential candidate's lack of foreign policy experience.

206. HYPERBOLE:

A figure of speech in which exaggeration is used for emphasis or effect; extreme exaggeration

Have you ever exaggerated something to make a point? Everyone does. In show business these exaggerations are called hype. In literature and daily life they are called HYPERBOLES. Here is a list of some commonly used HYPERBOLES:

- "I'm so tired that I could sleep for a year."

- "I'm so hungry that I could eat a horse."
- "This book weighs a ton."

207. CARICATURE:

A representation in which the subject's distinctive features or peculiarities are deliberately exaggerated for comic effect

Do you look at the editorial cartoons in your local newspaper? Editorial cartoonists often incorporate CARICATURES of political figures into their cartoons. For example, Thomas Nast's CARICATURES of Boss Tweed helped to focus public attention on the Tweed Ring's corrupt practices. Modern cartoonists often CARICATURE Jay Leno by exaggerating his already-prominent chin.

208. EPIC:

A long narrative poem written in a grand style to celebrate the feats of a legendary hero

SAGA:

A long narrative story; a heroic tale

Both EPICS and SAGAS are long and feature the feats of heroes. The two literary forms differ in that an EPIC is a narrative poem and a SAGA is a narrative story written in prose.

The *Iliad* is the first and greatest EPIC in Western literature. Other famous EPICS include Virgil's *Aeneid*, Homer's *The Odyssey*, and Milton's *Paradise Lost*. J.K. Rowling's series of seven Harry Potter novels provide a contemporary example of a literary SAGA while George Lucas' six Star Wars films provide a contemporary example of a cinematic SAGA.

209. EUPHONY:

Soothing or pleasant sounds; harmonious

CACOPHONY:

Harsh clashing sounds; jarring; grating

In their classic Motown song, "My Girl," The Temptations tell everyone who will listen that "I've got a sweeter song than the birds in the trees. Well I guess you'd say what can make me feel this way? My girl, talkin' 'bout my girl." The Temptations' soothing words and harmonious melody create a EUPH-ONIOUS sound. In contrast, Eminem describes his apprehension and fear before a make-or-break performance: "His palms are sweaty, knees weak, arms heavy. There's vomit on his sweater already, mom's spaghetti." Eminem's harsh grating words and rapid-fire rhythm create a CACOPHONOUS sound.

 Tip for a Direct Hit

EUPHONY and CACOPHONY are easy words to learn. Both include the Greek root *phone* meaning sound (like a cell phone). Since the prefix *eu* means "good," EUPHONY literally means "good sound." Since the prefix *kakos* means "bad," CACOPHONY means "bad sound."

210. FORESHADOW:

To suggest or indicate that something will happen in a story; PRESAGE (Word 301)

The conclusion of *Batman Begins* FORESHADOWS the Caped Crusader's coming battle with the Joker. As the film ends, Lieutenant Gordon unveils a Bat-Signal for Batman. He then mentions a criminal who, like Batman, has "a taste for the theatrical," leaving a Joker card at his crime scenes. Batman promises to investigate it, thus FORESHADOWING his coming confrontation with the Joker in *The Dark Knight*.

211. SUBPLOT:

A secondary plot in fiction or drama

SUBPLOTS are a common feature in novels and movies. For example, *The Great Gatsby* includes a SUBPLOT based upon the relationship between the narrator Nick Carraway and Jordan Baker, an attractive but CAPRICIOUS (Word 63) professional golfer. Similarly, the movie *Iron Man* includes a SUBPLOT hinting at a possible future romance between Tony Stark and his loyal assistant "Pepper" Potts.

212. MEMOIR:

An autobiography; personal journal

What do President Ulysses S. Grant, rapper 50 Cent, and rocker Anthony Kiedis have in common? All three wrote CANDID (open, honest) MEMOIRS describing their lives and careers. Written to pay off debts and provide for his family, the *Personal Memoirs of Ulysses S. Grant* is now considered the first and best presidential memoir. *From Pieces to Weight* is 50 Cent's unflinching MEMOIR chronicling his rise from

Jamaica, Queens to the top of the Billboard charts. *Scar Tissue* is Anthony Kiedis' account of his career as the lead singer of the Red Hot Chili Peppers.

213. ANECDOTE:

A short account of an interesting or humorous incident

What do the world-renowned physicist Albert Einstein and the lead singer of the Red Hot Chili Peppers, Anthony Kiedis, have in common? Both are very good at telling interesting ANECDOTES. In the following ANECDOTES, Einstein provides a humorous explanation of relativity, and Kiedis provides a revealing ANECDOTE of what it is like to be the opening act for the Rolling Stones:

> Albert Einstein was often asked to explain the general theory of relativity. "Put your hand on a hot stove for a minute, and it seems like an hour," he once declared. "Sit with a pretty girl for an hour, and it seems like a minute. That's relativity."

> "Opening for the Stones is a crummy job...First you get there and they won't let you do a sound check. Then they give you an eightieth of the stage. They set aside this tiny area and say, 'This is for you. You don't get the lights, and you're not allowed to use our sound system. And oh, by the way, you see that wooden floor? That's Mick's imported antique wood flooring from the Brazilian jungle, and that's what he dances on. If you so much as look at it, you won't get paid.'"

214. EULOGY:

A LAUDATORY (Word 91) speech or written tribute, especially one praising someone who has died

Here are three noteworthy EULOGIES:

- Mark Antony's fictional EULOGY for Julius Caesar in Shakespeare's play *Julius Caesar*

- Ossie Davis's EULOGY for Malcolm X

- Earl Spencer's eulogy for Diana, Princess of Wales

On the lighter side, in the movie *Zoolander*, Derek Zoolander delivered a EULOGY for his friends who died in the "Orange Mocha Frappuccino" gas fight.

215. ALLUSION:

An indirect or brief reference to a person, event, place, phrase, piece of art, or literary work that assumes a common knowledge with the reader or listener

Many contemporary songs and TV shows contain clever ALLUSIONS to works of literature. For example, in her song "Love Story," Taylor Swift makes ALLUSIONS to Shakespeare's play *Romeo and Juliet* and Hawthorne's novel *Scarlet Letter* when she warns her romantic lover, "Cause you were Romeo, I was a scarlet letter." The TV show *Gossip Girl* often uses literary ALLUSIONS in the title of its episodes. For example, the episode "The Serena Also Rises" is an ALLUSION to Hemingway's novel *The Sun Also Rises*.

Testing Your Vocabulary

Each SAT contains 19 sentence completion questions and 48 critical reading questions. While the words in this chapter are used infrequently in sentence completions, they often appear in critical reading questions. Always remember that each passage will contain key words and phrases that will lead you to the correct answer. Use the vocabulary from Chapter 6 to answer the following 5 critical reading questions and make sure to circle your answers. You'll find answers and explanations on pages 16-17.

While critics panned Laurie's essays as too arcane for the average reader, they rushed to praise Madison's new novel. According to her legion of adoring fans, Madison writes in a hip, contemporary style, full of topical pop culture references. Thus, she writes knowingly about Miley Cyrus' latest song, Patrick Dempsey's latest movie and Rick Ross's latest chain and piece. As a result, Madison is being universally praised as a promising new talent.

1. Lines 5 – 8 ("Thus, she ... piece") serve to provide examples of

    (A) particular references that critics found too esoteric

    (B) diverse subjects about which Madison has only superficial knowledge

    (C) comic subplots that enhance the novel's core theme

    (D) anecdotes that illustrate key ideas

    (E) specific allusions in Madison's novel

In the movie *300*, director Zach Snyder compares Sparta to a lonely citadel of freedom valiantly holding out against the tyrant Xerxes and his vast horde of Persian soldiers. This heroic image of indomitable Spartans determined to fight to the death remains dominant in popular culture. Without slighting Sparta's contribution to the defense of ancient Greece, it is important to remember that it was the Athenians who sacrificed their city and then defeated the Persian fleet at the watershed battle of Platea.

2. The author suggests that the "lonely citadel of freedom" (line 2) is best understood as

   (A) an anecdote relaying an important message
   (B) an unflattering flashback
   (C) a vivid metaphor for heroic resistance
   (D) a satirical commentary on Spartan bravery
   (E) an uninspired simile

In her novel, *The Women of Brewster Place*, Gloria Naylor describes Etta Johnson's deliberately conspicuous arrival at Brewster Place: "The apple-green car with the white vinyl roof and Florida plates turned into the street like a greased cobra. Since Etta had stopped at a Mobil station three blocks away to work off the evidence of a hot, dusty 1,200-mile odyssey home, the chrome caught the rays of the afternoon sun and shone brightly like a gaudy neon sign."

3. Lines 3 – 8 ("The apple-green...sign") are notable for their use of

   (A) wry wit
   (B) vivid similes
   (C) biting satire
   (D) obscure allusions
   (E) illuminating anecdotes

As a young boy, I beamed with pride as college students described my father's economics lectures. Everyone praised his vivid anecdotes, amusing stories and vast storehouse of economic data that he could marshal at a moment's notice. The "Professor," as everyone called him, even appeared as a guest pundit on a local television program. The first time I saw dad I was shocked and embarrassed. The bright lights and heavy makeup exaggerated his bushy eyebrows and lit up his bald head. The same darting eyes that mesmerized his students gave him the appearance of one of the villains I watched on the Sunday morning cartoon shows.

4. In lines 6 – 12 ("The first time ... shows"), the narrator suggests that, on television, his father came across as a

    (A) caricature
    (B) knowledgeable commentator
    (C) self-deprecating authority
    (D) ironic and tragic figure
    (E) raconteur

Mr. Williams praised Alex's short story for its descriptive vocabulary and impressive use of metaphorical language. However, as an honest and incisive critic, Mr. Williams admonished Alex for failing to explore the relationship between the literal meaning of what his protagonist said and what he really implied.

5. Mr. Williams criticized Alex's short story for its

    (A)   outstanding use of metaphors and similes
    (B)   magisterial tone
    (C)   incoherent structure
    (D)   lack of dramatic irony
    (E)   unrealistic hyperboles

Answers and Explanations

1. **E**

    An ALLUSION (Word 215) is an indirect or brief reference to a person, place or event. The passage notes that Madison's writing is filled with examples of "topical pop culture references." Since these references are specific allusions, the correct answer is E, "specific allusions in Madison's novel."

2. **C**

    A METAPHOR (Word 202) is a figure of speech comparing two unlike things. Director Zack Snyder compares Sparta to a "lonely citadel of freedom valiantly holding out against the tyrant Xerxes..." The correct answer is therefore C, "a vivid metaphor for heroic resistance."

3. **B**

    A SIMILE (Word 202) is a figure of speech using like or as to compare two unlike things. Gloria Naylor uses similes when she writes that the Etta's car was "like a greased cobra" and that the car's chrome "shone brightly like a gaudy neon sign." The correct answer is therefore B, "vivid similes."

4. **A**

    A CARICATURE (Word 207) is a deliberately exaggerated portrait. The key word "exaggerates" signals that the description of the narrator's father is in fact a caricature. The correct answer is therefore A, "caricature."

5. **D**

IRONY (Word 204) is used to describe a situation in which things are not what they are said to be or what they seem. Mr. Williams criticized Alex for not fully exploring "the discrepancy between the literal meaning of what his protagonists said and what he really implied." Mr. Williams thus underscored Alex's failure to use dramatic irony. The correct answer is therefore D, "lack of dramatic irony."

Chapter 7

SCIENCE AND THE SOCIAL SCIENCES: 216–260

Many students believe that SAT words are obscure and rarely used by anyone except test writers at the Educational Testing Service. Nothing could be further from the truth. Newspapers, magazines, and Internet blogs frequently use SAT vocabulary words. Front page headlines describe "watershed events," financial articles discuss "lucrative deals," and editorials urge politicians to "reach a consensus" on important issues.

This chapter highlights 45 key words taken from science and the social sciences. While all appear on the SAT, they are also all everyday words that you encounter in school and on the internet. Since memorizing lists is inefficient and ineffective, we have provided vivid examples designed to help you make a permanent connection with each word.

A. SCIENCE: THESE WORDS WILL HELP YOU DESCRIBE WHAT IS HAPPENING IN THE SCIENCE LAB

216. CATALYST:

In chemistry, a CATALYST is a substance (such as an enzyme) that accelerates the rate of a chemical reaction at some temperature, but without itself being transformed or consumed by the reaction. In everyday usage a CATALYST is any agent that provokes or triggers change.

Both Rosa Parks and Rachel Carson were CATALYSTS whose actions helped provoke historic changes. Rosa Parks' refusal to give up her bus seat acted as a CATALYST that helped spark the Montgomery Bus Boycott. Today, Rosa Parks is hailed as one of the pioneers of the modern civil rights movement. Rachel Carson's book *Silent Spring* was a CATALYST that triggered a national campaign to limit the indiscriminate use of DDT and other harmful pesticides. Today, Rachel Carson is hailed as one of the pioneers of the modern environmental movement.

217. CAUSTIC:

In chemistry, a CAUSTIC substance is one that burns or destroys organic tissue by chemical action. Hydrofluoric acid and silver nitrate are examples of CAUSTIC substances. In everyday usage, a CAUSTIC comment is one that hurts or burns.

In the movie *Ever After*, Danielle asked her wicked step-mother, "Was there ever a time, even in its smallest measure, when you loved me?" The insensitive step-mother replied, "How can anyone love a pebble in their shoe?" Ouch! Now that was a CAUSTIC remark!

As a judge on *American Idol*, Simon Cowell was famous for the CAUSTIC barbs he directed at INEPT (Word 114) contestants. For example, he told one would-be singer, "If your lifeguard duties were as good as your singing, a lot of people would be drowning." Ouch! Now that was a CAUSTIC remark!

218. CRYSTALLIZE:

In chemistry, CRYSTALLIZE is the process by which crystals are formed. In everyday usage, CRYSTALLIZE means to give a definite form to an idea or plan

In both the classic TV show and the recent movie, the A-Team was a fictional group of soldiers of fortune led by John "Hannibal" Smith. Hannibal was especially pleased when one of his elaborate ideas CRYSTALLIZED into a successful plan. Like the WILY (clever) Hannibal, you must be METICULOUS (Word 8) as you design a plan to ace the SAT. In addition to studying *Direct Hits*, you might also check out "Silverturtle's Guide to SAT and Admissions Success" at CollegeConfidential.com. Silverturtle does a great job of CRYSTALLIZING valuable information.

219. OSMOSIS:

In chemistry, OSMOSIS refers to the diffusion of a fluid through a semi-permeable membrane until there is an equal concentration of fluid on both sides of the membrane. In everyday usage, OSMOSIS refers to a gradual, often unconscious process of assimilation.

What do students studying for the SAT and the Holy Roman Emperor Charlemagne have in common? Charlemagne valued education and tried so hard to study Latin that he had tablets with vocabulary words placed under his pillow. Charlemagne apparently hoped he could learn difficult words by OSMOSIS. Like Charlemagne, modern SAT students have to learn difficult new words. But don't put this book under your pillow. OSMOSIS didn't work for Charlemagne, and it won't work for you! The words in this book can only be learned by studying and using them.

220. SEDENTARY:

In ecology, animals that are SEDENTARY remain or live in one area. In everyday usage, SEDENTARY means settled and therefore accustomed to sitting or doing little exercise

What do fungus beetles and the humans in the movie *WALL-E* have in common? Both live SEDENTARY lives. Fungus beetles are SEDENTARY creatures that seldom move more than a few yards between fungi, their primary food. The humans in *WALL-E* are 28th century couch potatoes who spend most of their time reclining in chairs while staring at computer screens. As a result of this SEDENTARY lifestyle, the humans are CORPULENT (overweight, obese) and have almost lost the ability to walk.

221. VIRULENT:

In medical science, VIRULENT refers to a disease or toxin that is extremely infectious, malignant, or poisonous. In everyday usage, VIRULENT refers to language that is bitterly hostile, hateful, and antagonistic

What do the blue-ringed octopus and the hook-nosed sea snake have in common? Both are DIMINUTIVE (Word 51) animals whose venom is extremely VIRULENT. Although only the size of a golf ball, the blue-ringed octopus can kill an adult human in minutes with its VIRULENT venom. Armed with venom four to eight times more VIRULENT than that of a cobra, the hook-nosed sea snake can easily kill almost any animal that encroaches on its territory.

The blue-ringed octopus and the hook-nosed sea snake use their VIRULENT venom to protect themselves from predators. In contrast, Al Qaeda terrorists regularly broadcast VIRULENT speeches directed at the innocent citizens of democratic nations.

222. EMPIRICAL:

In science, EMPIRICAL means originating in or based on direct observation and experience. EMPIRICAL data can then be used to support or reject a hypothesis. In everyday language, EMPIRICAL means to be guided by practical experience, not theory.

The process of applying to colleges can be a DAUNTING (intimidating) challenge. You should begin your search with a series of questions: Would you prefer to go to an urban college or one in a more BUCOLIC (Word 79) setting? Would you be more comfortable in a large state university or a small private college? These questions are only a first step.

It is very important to be EMPIRICAL, to gather facts. Don't speculate about what a college is like or what test scores you will need. Be an EMPIRICIST and visit a number of colleges. On your visit, gather EMPIRICAL information by visiting dorms, observing classes, talking with students, and asking questions.

223. ENTOMOLOGY:
The scientific study of insects

How are honeybees, strawberry ice cream, ENTOMOLOGISTS, and the SAT connected? Honeybees are responsible for pollinating one-third of all the foods we eat including strawberries, blueberries, apples, almonds, and melons. Without honeybees, all-natural strawberry ice cream would be impossible to make. The last several winters have witnessed the sudden disappearance of more than 25 percent of the Western honeybee population. ENTOMOLOGISTS are MYSTIFIED (baffled) by what is officially called colony collapse disorder.

 Tip for a Direct Hit

While SAT test writers may or may not be aware of the problem facing honeybees, they are aware that many students confuse ENTOMOLOGY with ETYMOLOGY. ENTOMOLOGY is the study of insects while ETYMOLOGY is a branch of linguistics concerned with the history of words.

224. GESTATE:

In science, GESTATE means to carry within the uterus from conception to delivery. In everyday language, GESTATE means to conceive and develop in the mind

Periods of GESTATION vary from animal to animal. For example, the period of GESTATION for domesticated cats and dogs is two months. In contrast, the period of GESTATION for elephants is almost 22 months!

Ideas, like a fetus, often require time to GESTATE. For example, the ideas contained in the Declaration of Independence did not suddenly spring from Jefferson's mind onto a piece of parchment. He later acknowledged that his eloquent statements about natural rights were derived from the English philosopher John Locke and had been GESTATING in his mind for some time.

225. PARADIGM:

In science, a PARADIGM is a framework or model of thought

In 1610, the Italian astronomer and physicist Galileo Galilei did something no other human being had ever done before. He pointed a telescope at Jupiter and observed the orbits of four of its moons. Galileo realized the force (which we now call gravity) that kept the moons of Jupiter in their orbits was the same force keeping the Earth and the other planets in their orbits around the Sun. Galileo's scientific observations refuted the old geocentric PARADIGM that the Sun and all the planets revolve around the Earth. Instead,

Galileo offered scientific support for Copernicus' revolutionary new heliocentric PARADIGM that placed the Sun in the center of the solar system. Galileo's work triggered a MOMENTOUS (Word 193) PARADIGM shift in human thought.

B.   ECONOMICS: THESE WORDS ARE ABOUT DOLLARS AND SENSE

226. ENTREPRENEUR:

A person who organizes and manages a business or enterprise

Mark Zuckerberg is an American ENTREPRENEUR who is the co-founder of Facebook. Zuckerberg launched Facebook from his Harvard dorm room on February 4, 2004. Facebook now has over 500 million users and generates over $1 billion in revenue. As a result, Zuckerberg is one of the youngest billionaires in the world.

Although Zuckerberg is an ENTREPRENEUR, he is not an INNOVATOR (Word 126). Zuckerberg borrowed his original concept from a product produced by his prep school Phillips Exeter Academy. For decades, the school published and distributed a printed manual for all its students and faculty, unofficially called the "face book." However, Zuckerberg was PRESCIENT (Word 365). Like other Internet pioneers, he understood the power of the Web to create an interactive community of users.

227. LUCRATIVE:
Very profitable

Actors COVET (Word 32) lead roles in popular TV programs. In addition to fame, starring roles are also rewarded with LUCRATIVE salaries. For example, Hugh Laurie, the start of *House M.D.* earns $400,000 per episode. While established stars command the most LUCRATIVE salaries, newcomers can also expect big paychecks. For example, Matthew Morrison (*Glee*) and Nicole "Snooki" Polizzi (*Jersey Shore*) both earn $30,000 per episode.

228. EXTRAVAGANT:
Excessive and therefore lacking restraint

The Bugatti Veyron EB 16.4 is the world's most powerful and EXTRAVAGANT car. The Veyron's 1001 horsepower engine can accelerate from 0 to 62 mph in just 2.46 seconds making it the fastest street-legal production car in the world. Of course, the Veyron also consumes an EXTRAVAGANT amount of fuel, using just under 6 mpg in city driving. At full throttle, the Veyron would empty its 26-gallon fuel tank in just 12 minutes. How much does this EXTRAVAGANT car cost? It can be yours for $1,700,000!

229. AVARICE:
Excessive desire for material wealth; greedy; covetous

Philosophers and religious leaders have long condemned AVARICE. The Greek philosopher Aristotle demonstrated his deep understanding of human nature when he wrote, "The AVARICE of mankind is insatiable." During the Middle Ages, Christian theologians identified AVARICE as one of the seven deadly sins. Sculptors often showed AVARICIOUS moneylenders being tortured by demons while clutching bags filled with coins.

While theologians have long denounced AVARICE, it does have defenders in the world of high finance. In the movie *Wall Street*, Gordon Gekko was an AVARICIOUS corporate raider. He vigorously advocated AVARICE when he proclaimed, "greed is good. Greed works, greed is right ... Greed for life, money, love, knowledge, has marked the upward surge of mankind – and greed, mark my words, will save the malfunctioning corporation called the U.S.A."

230. GLUT, PLETHORA, SURFEIT:
A surplus

While our used-car lots now have a GLUT of gas-guzzling vehicles, our landfills are filling up with a PLETHORA of old computers, printers, TVs, and other unwanted consumer electronic goods. Americans are now throwing away two million tons of electronic trash, or e-waste, each year. While there is a SURFEIT of outdated e-waste, there is currently a PAUCITY (Word 4) of recycling options. The Environmental Protection Agency estimates that we only recycle 350,000 tons of e-waste each year.

231. DESTITUTE, IMPOVERISHED, INDIGENT:
Very poor

AFFLUENT and OPULENT:
Very wealthy

In the movie *Trading Places*, Eddie Murphy's character was originally DESTITUTE but became very AFFLUENT. In the movie *Coming to America*, Murphy played an African prince who pretended to be IMPOVERISHED but had in fact grown up in an OPULENT palace.

Eddie Murphy's characters were both fictional. In the movie *The Pursuit of Happyness*, Will Smith portrayed the real life story of how Chris Gardner lost all of his family's savings by investing in a franchise selling bone density scanners. As a result, Chris became INDIGENT, forcing him and his young son to spend nights riding buses and sleeping in subway restrooms. Chris ultimately became AFFLUENT by learning how to become a successful stock broker.

232. MUNIFICENT:
Very generous

What do Oprah Winfrey, Angelina Jolie, and Brad Pitt have in common? All three are celebrities known for their MUNIFICENT donations to charities. Oprah is the world's most MUNIFICENT celebrity donor. In 2008, she donated $50 million, nearly 20 percent of the $275 million she earned. Angelina Jolie and Brad Pitt came in second, giving $8.4 million to their Jolie-Pitt Foundation. The couple donated one-fourth of the $34 million they earned. Their LARGESSE (generosity) will enable the Make It Right Project to build 150 green houses in New Orleans.

233. PARSIMONIOUS:
Excessively cheap with money; stingy

Would you want people to call you a "Scrooge?" You probably would not. Ebenezer Scrooge is the leading character in *A Christmas Carol* by Charles Dickens. Scrooge lived up to his name by being very PARSIMONIOUS. A PARSIMONIOUS person would be the ANTITHESIS (Word 33) of someone who is MUNIFICENT (Word 232).

234. DEPRECIATION:
Any decrease or loss in value caused by age, wear, or market conditions

DEPRECIATION means that values are going down! The stock market Crash of 1929 caused a severe DEPRECIATION in the value of stocks. By 1932, stocks listed on the New York Stock Exchange were worth just 11 percent of their pre-Crash value. DEPRECIATION is not limited to historic examples found only in textbooks. In 2008, American homeowners collectively lost more than $2 trillion in home value as their properties DEPRECIATED by an average of 8.4 percent.

235. REMUNERATE:
To compensate; to make payment for; to pay a person

REMUNERATION varies greatly from job to job. On July 24, 2009, the Federal minimum wage rose from $6.55 per hour to $7.25 per hour. The President of the

United States earns $400,000 per year, and the Vice-President earns $227,300. In contrast, Tiger Woods is the top paid athlete in the world, having earned approximately $110 million dollars in 2010.

C. HISTORY AND GEOGRAPHY: THESE WORDS WILL HELP YOU UNDERSTAND PEOPLE, PLACES AND EVENTS

236. ACCORD:
A formal agreement

In *Pirates of the Caribbean: The Curse of the Black Pearl*, Captain Jack Sparrow and Will reach an ACCORD. Will agreed to free Sparrow, and Sparrow agreed to help Will find Elizabeth. In world affairs, nations also sign ACCORDS. For example, the Helsinki ACCORDS (1975) recognized basic human rights, and the Camp David ACCORDS (1978) provided a framework for establishing peaceful relations between Egypt and Israel.

237. ENLIGHTEN:
To inform, instruct, illuminate, and thus remove darkness and ignorance

During the Enlightenment, writers such as Voltaire ENLIGHTENED European society by urging people to use science and reason instead of blindly following inherited prejudices. In cartoons and comics, why do you think a light-bulb appears over someone's head when the person suddenly understands something? Because they are ENLIGHTENED!

238. APPEASEMENT:
The policy of granting concessions to maintain peace

Would you APPEASE a crying child by giving him or her a piece of candy? Would you APPEASE a bully who threatened to beat you up? Are there times when APPEASEMENT is a wise policy? The British Prime Minister Neville Chamberlain thought so. At the Munich Conference in September 1938, Chamberlain APPEASED Hitler by agreeing to his demand to control the Sudetenland. When he returned to London, Chamberlain told cheering crowds, "I believe it is peace for our time." Chamberlain's prediction proved to be tragically wrong.

239. NULLIFY:
To make null; declare invalid

The tariffs of 1828 and 1832 infuriated John C. Calhoun of South Carolina. Led by Calhoun, South Carolina voted to NULLIFY or invalidate the tariffs. President Jackson rejected NULLIFICATION by saying that it was treason and that those implementing it were traitors. The crisis was averted when Henry Clay devised a compromise in which the tariffs were gradually lowered.

240. TRIUMVIRATE:
A group or association of three leaders

John C. Calhoun, Henry Clay (See Word 239), and Daniel Webster were a group of three American statesmen known as "The Great Triumvirate," who dominated the U.S. Senate during the 1830s and 1840s. While the term TRIUMVIRATE usually refers to political leaders, it can be used to describe any group of three (remember, the prefix *tri* means three). For example, the videogame console market is dominated by the TRIUMVIRATE of Nintendo's Wii, Sony's PlayStation 3, and Microsoft's Xbox 360.

241. PRETEXT:
An excuse; an alleged cause

On August 2 and 4, 1964, two American destroyers patrolling international waters in the Gulf of Tonkin reported that they had been fired upon by North Vietnamese PT boats. While later investigations strongly suggested that the North Vietnamese fired in self-defense on August 2 and the "attack" of August 4 never happened, President Johnson used the alleged attacks as a PRETEXT to ask Congress for broader powers. The PRETEXT worked. Congress promptly passed the *Tonkin Gulf Resolution*, giving Johnson a blank check to escalate the war in Southeast Asia.

242. WATERSHED:
Critical point that marks a change of course; a turning point

Each generation of Americans has experienced a WATERSHED event that has riveted the entire nation and has marked a crucial historic turning point. On January 20, 2009, a record crowd of approximately 1.5 million people watched Chief Justice John Roberts swear-in Barack Obama as the 44th President of the United States. The inauguration marked a historic WATERSHED in American history as Obama became America's first African-American president. For millions of people in the United States and around the world, the inauguration marked the fulfillment of Dr. King's dream and the beginning of a new era in American political history.

243. CONSENSUS:
A general agreement

Do you think there is a need to develop and use more alternative energy sources? If you answer yes to this question, you are part of a growing national CONSENSUS on this issue. Soaring gasoline prices have forced Americans to realize that we cannot indefinitely continue to import 70 percent of our oil at an annual cost of $700 billion. Note that a CONSENSUS does not mean that everyone must be in complete agreement with a policy or a decision. While there is a CONSENSUS that America must develop new sources of energy, there is not yet a CONSENSUS on which of the MYRIAD (Word 323) proposed alternative energy solutions should be utilized.

244. AUTOCRAT and DESPOT:
A ruler having unlimited power

In the movie *300*, Xerxes is portrayed as an AUTOCRAT who is determined to conquer and enslave the freedom-loving Greeks. However, led by Sparta and Athens, the Greeks successfully defeat Xerxes, thus defending democracy. Although democracy continues to make great strides, the modern world still has countries ruled by AUTOCRATS. For example, Kim Jong Il wields absolute power over North Korea. Known to his people as "The Dear Leader," the AUTOCRATIC Kim brutally suppresses dissidents and maintains the world's fourth largest army. While his IM-POVERISHED (Word 231) people suffer from repeated famines, their DESPOTIC "Dear Leader" dines on steak and sips expensive imported wines.

245. MANIFESTO:
A public declaration of beliefs, policies or intentions

MANIFESTOS are not written by people who are self-satisfied and complacent. They are written by people who are INDIGNANT (Word 65) and demand a change. For example, in 1848, a small but determined group of feminists held a Women's Rights Convention at Seneca Falls, New York. Led by the defiant Elizabeth Cady Stanton, they issued a MANIFESTO called the "Declaration of Sentiments," which boldly declared that "all men and women are created equal." The MANIFESTO launched the modern women's rights movement.

246. ENFRANCHISE:
To receive the right to vote

DISENFRANCHISE:
To lose the right to vote

In American history, Jim Crow laws DISENFRAN-CHISED African-American voters, while the Voting Rights Act of 1965 ENFRANCHISED African-American voters. Ratified in 1920, the Nineteenth Amendment ENFRANCHISED millions of American women. The 26th Amendment ENFRANCHISED 18-year-old American citizens.

247. COERCE:

To force to act or think in a certain way by use of pressure, threats, or torture; to compel

Joseph Stalin ruled the Soviet Union as an AUTOCRAT (Word 244) from 1924 until his death in 1953. Stalin used terror to COERCE the Russian people to unquestioningly follow his leadership. In the *Gulag Archipelago*, Alexander Solzhenitsyn describes a Communist Party conference in which officials respond to a call for a tribute to Comrade Stalin with "stormy applause." The ovation continued because secret police "were standing in the hall applauding and waiting to see who would quit first!" The threat of COERCION worked: "The applause went on-six, seven, eight minutes! They were done for!" Finally after 11 minutes the director of a paper factory stopped applauding and sat down. But that, Solzhenitsyn explains, "Was how they discovered who the independent people were." In a frightening demonstration of COERCION, the authorities arrested the factory director and sentenced him to ten years in a labor camp. In a chilling reminder of the power of a totalitarian state to COERCE conformity, the interrogator reminded the former factory director, "Don't ever be the first to stop applauding."

248. EGALITARIAN:

Favoring social equality; belief in a society in which all people have equal political, economic, and civil rights

During the nineteenth century, American utopian leaders were inspired by a dream of creating EGALIT-ARIAN communities. Founded by John Humphrey

Noyes, the Oneida Community in upstate New York became a flourishing EGALITARIAN commonwealth of some 300 people. Men and women shared equally in all the community's tasks, from field to factory to kitchen. The members lived in one building and ate in a common dining hall. The dream of EGALITARIAN living did not last. The communal dining hall ultimately became a restaurant where meals were bought with money. Led by Noyes's son, Pierrepont, Oneida Community, Ltd. grew into the world's leading manufacturer of stainless steel knives, forks, and spoons with annual sales of a half billion dollars.

249. DEMARCATION:
The setting or marking of boundaries or limits as a line of demarcation

What is the relationship between the SAT word DEMARCATION and the reason why Brazil is the only Portuguese-speaking country in the Americas? Columbus' WATERSHED (Word 242) voyage created an ACRIMONIOUS (Word 196) dispute between Spain and Portugal over the rights to lands in the New World. The two nations avoided an IMPASSE (Word 28) by agreeing to the 1494 Treaty of Tordesillas. Under the terms of this agreement, Spain and Portugal divided the non-Christian world into two zones of influence. The line of DEMARCATION gave Portugal a claim to Brazil.

Tip for a Direct Hit

The Latin word *bellum* means "war." So a BELLICOSE statement would be warlike and hostile in manner. U.S. history students will recognize *bellum* in the term ANTEBELLUM, meaning the period before the Civil War. And Harry Potter fans will recognize *bellum* in the name Bellatrix Lestrange. In ancient Rome, a *bellatrix* was a female warrior. Bellatrix Lestrange more than lived up to her name. She was a particularly BELLICOSE follower of Lord Voldemort.

250. INQUISITION:
A severe interrogation; a systematic questioning

The INQUISITION was a formal court of justice established by the Roman Catholic Church (1232-1820) to discover and suppress HERESY (false beliefs). Although the United States has never had a formal court of INQUISITION, numerous zealots have conducted INQUISITIONS into the conduct of public officials. The best known of these INQUISITIONS was conducted by Senator McCarthy during the early 1950s. McCarthy ruthlessly questioned public officials as part of his campaign against alleged Communists. Instigated by McCarthyism, Hollywood "blacklists" unfairly STIGMATIZED (branded) screen writers, actors, and directors as Communist sympathizers.

251. AMELIORATE:

To make a situation better

EXACERBATE:

To make a situation worse

What do Dorothea Dix, Ida B. Wells-Barnett, and Batman have in common? All three were crusaders who dedicated themselves to AMELIORATING social problems. Dorothea Dix worked to AMELIORATE the lives of the INDIGENT (Word 231) insane by creating the first generation of American mental hospitals. Ida B. Wells-Barnett worked to AMELIORATE the lives of African-Americans by exposing the problem of lynching in the South. And Batman worked to AMELIORATE the lives of the citizens of Gotham City by fighting the power of its crime bosses. Interestingly, Batman learned PARADOXICALLY (Word 41) that his efforts also EXACERBATED Gotham's crime problem by leading to an escalation of violence.

252. CONTIGUOUS:

Sharing an edge or boundary; touching

Which of the following is the southernmost city in the 48 CONTIGUOUS states?

(A) Kaalualu, Hawaii
(B) Key West, Florida

The answer depends upon the meaning of the word CONTIGUOUS. Since the 48 CONTIGUOUS or touching states do not include Hawaii (or Alaska), the correct answer is B. Hawaii is actually an ARCHIPELAGO (chain of islands) located in the central Pacific Ocean about 2,000 miles southwest of the 48 CONTIGUOUS states.

Tip for a Direct Hit

The words CONTIGUOUS and PROXIMITY are easy to confuse. CONTIGUOUS means that two objects actually touch. In contrast, PROXIMITY means that two objects are very near in space or time. On a city street, two CONTIGUOUS businesses touch each other, while two businesses separated by other stores share a close PROXIMITY to each other.

253. DESICCATE:
Thoroughly dried out; lifeless, totally arid

Antarctica is technically a desert that receives less than two inches of precipitation a year. One interior region of the Antarctic is known as the Dry Valleys. These valleys have not seen rainfall in over two million years. The Dry Valleys exist because 100 mph Katabatic downwinds DESICCATE all moisture. The freezing temperatures and the absence of water and all life simulate conditions on the Planet Mars. As a result, the region is used as a training ground for astronauts who may one day make a voyage to the equally-DESICCATED Red Planet.

D. LAW AND ORDER: THESE WORDS WILL HELP YOU UNDERSTAND HOW THE WHEELS OF JUSTICE TURN

254. PERTINENT:
Relevant; to the point; a clear illustration of a major point

In the movie *Remember the Titans*, Gerry criticizes Julius for not listening to his coaches and for selfish play. Julius defends himself by asking Gerry these PERTINENT questions: "Why should I give a hoot about you or anybody else out there? You are the Captain, right? Then why don't you tell your white buddies to block for Rev or Plugged Nickel? I'm supposed to wear myself out for the team. What team?" Gerry reacts by saying "That's the worst attitude I ever heard," but Julius responds with a PERTINENT point: "Attitude reflects leadership, Captain."

255. COMPLICITY:
Association or participation in a wrongful act

Tupac Shakur is widely believed to be America's greatest and most successful rapper with 75 million albums sold worldwide and over 50 million in the United States. On September 7, 1996, Shakur was shot four times in a drive-by shooting in Las Vegas. He died six days later. Because of their bitter rivalry with Tupac, rappers Biggie Smalls and Sean Combs were suspected of COMPLICITY in the murder. However, both Biggie and Combs vigorously denied any COMPLICITY in Tupac's death. Despite many investigations, the case remains unsolved.

256. EXONERATE and EXCULPATE:
Both mean to free from guilt or blame

What do Benjamin Franklin Gates (*National Treasure: Book of Secrets*) and Harry Potter have in common? They both EXONERATED members of their families of EXECRABLE (Word 364) crimes. Ben successfully EXCULPATED his great-great-grand-father, Thomas Gates, of COMPLICITY (Word 255) in the plot to assassinate Abraham Lincoln. Harry successfully EXONERATED his godfather Sirius Black of the murder of Peter Pettigrew and 12 Muggles.

257. INDISPUTABLE:
Not open to question; undeniable; irrefutable

Who killed President Kennedy? The Warren Commission published a comprehensive report providing what it believed was INDISPUTABLE evidence that Lee Harvey Oswald acted alone. However, SKEPTICS (Word 102) soon criticized the Warren Commission's findings. In the movie *JFK*, director Oliver Stone presents what he considers INDISPUTABLE evidence that Lee Harvey Oswald was in fact part of a secret conspiracy to kill President Kennedy.

258. PRECEDENT:
An act or instance that is used as an example in dealing with subsequent similar instances

Suppose you were part of a group scheduled to visit the White House and meet the President. How would you address the President and, upon meeting him (or her), what would you do? These issues have been settled by long-established PRECEDENTS. Washington rejected "His Highness" and "His High Mightiness" for the simple greeting "Mr. President." After saying "Mr. President, it is an honor to meet you," would you bow or shake hands? Although Washington favored bowing, Thomas Jefferson felt the practice was too royal. He established the PRECEDENT of shaking hands, feeling that this gesture was more democratic.

259. UNPRECEDENTED:

Without previous example; an UNPREC-EDENTED event has never happened before

What do Tiger Woods and Will Smith have in common? Both have achieved UNPRECEDENTED success in their careers. Tiger Woods is on course to become the first billionaire athlete. It is interesting to note that prize money only accounts for about one-tenth of Tiger's earnings, with the rest coming from LUCRATIVE (Word 227) endorsements. Like Tiger, Will Smith has achieved UNPRECEDENTED success. As a result of the popularity of *Hancock*, Smith now has a streak of eight consecutive movies that have grossed over $100 million in ticket sales. This UNPRECEDENTED achievement establishes Will Smith as Hollywood's most marketable movie star.

260. MALFEASANCE:

Misconduct or wrongdoing, especially by a public official

On January 29, 2009, the Illinois state Senate convicted Governor Rod Blagojevich of numerous charges of MALFEASANCE. FBI phone wiretaps recorded Blagojevich BLATANTLY (unmistakably) discussing the possibility of selling the U.S. Senate seat vacated by the then-President-elect Barack Obama. "The seat," the governor said, "is a valuable thing; you don't just give it away for nothing." Blagojevich's MALFEASANCE did not stop with soliciting bids for a vacant Senate seat. He also abused his power by withholding an $8 million appropriation for a children's hospital unless the hospital's chief executive came through with an anticipated campaign contribution.

Testing Your Vocabulary

Each SAT contains 19 sentence completion questions that are primarily a test of your vocabulary. Each sentence completion will always have a key word or phrase that will lead you to the correct answer. Use the vocabulary from Chapters 6-7 to circle the answer to each of the following 10 sentence completion questions. You'll find answers and explanations on pages 48-49.

1. Museum officials hailed the patron's gift as both _____ and _____: it was very generous and without previous example.

    (A) ironic .. pertinent
    (B) munificent .. unprecedented
    (C) extravagant .. egalitarian
    (D) parsimonious .. enlightened
    (E) belligerent .. empirical

2. The new labor contract was reached by _____ and compromise, not by force and _____.

    (A) allusion .. hyperbole
    (B) malfeasance .. manifesto
    (C) avarice .. disenfranchisement
    (D) consensus .. coercion
    (E) osmosis .. appeasement

3.   The revolutionary leaders produced _____ that both clearly and succinctly declared their major beliefs while calling upon their followers to rise up against their oppressors.

   (A)   a memoir
   (B)   a manifesto
   (C)   a caricature
   (D)   a pretext
   (E)   an anecdote

4.   The forceful personality and generous patronage of Pope Julius II acted as _____, triggering an outpouring of artistic creativity now known as the High Renaissance.

   (A)   a pretext
   (B)   a metaphor
   (C)   a catalyst
   (D)   an allusion
   (E)   an accord

5.   Approved in 1920, the 19th Amendment _____ millions of American women who had been denied the right to vote since the ratification of the Constitution in 1789.

   (A)   enfranchised
   (B)   depreciated
   (C)   remunerated
   (D)   enlightened
   (E)   nullified

6. The storming of the Bastille on July 14, 1789, represents _____ event in French history, forever marking the end of the ancient regime and the beginning of a new democratic order.

   (A) an ironic
   (B) an empirical
   (C) a contiguous
   (D) a parsimonius
   (E) a watershed

7. Shilpa's _____ was the antithesis of her brother's generosity: she was very greedy, while he was very _____.

   (A) destitution .. affluence
   (B) irrelevance .. pertinent
   (C) inquisitiveness .. indifferent
   (D) egalitarianism .. autocratic
   (E) avarice .. munificent

8. The mayor's chief of staff successfully cleared herself of charges of _____ by proving that a member of the town council had clandestinely misappropriated the missing funds.

   (A) belligerence
   (B) appeasement
   (C) malfeasance
   (D) destitution
   (E) caricature

9. Critics justifiably charged that Getlein's _____ leanings would eventually undermine the company's _____ culture, which had always prized an open and nonhierarchical structure.

    (A) entrepreneurial .. creative
    (B) parsimonious .. inquisitive
    (C) empirical .. enlightened
    (D) sedentary .. consensus
    (E) autocratic .. egalitarian

10. Initially confined to a remote mountain village, the disease proved to be remarkably _____ as it infected people throughout the entire country.

    (A) virulent
    (B) remunerative
    (C) sedentary
    (D) caustic
    (E) complicitous

Answers and Explanations

1. **B**

   The question asks you to find a first word that means "very generous" and a second word that means "without previous example." The correct answer is MUNIFICENT (Word 232) and UNPRECEDENTED (Word 259).

2. **D**

   The question asks you to find a first word that is consistent with "compromise" and a second word that is consistent with "force." Since compromise and force are antonyms, the answer must also be a pair of antonyms. The correct answer is CONSENSUS (Word 243) and COERCION (Word 247).

3. **B**

   The question asks you to find a word describing a public declaration of beliefs. The correct answer is MANIFESTO (Word 245).

4. **C**

   The question asks you to find a word meaning "triggering." The correct answer is CATALYST (Word 216).

5. **A**

   The question asks you to find a word that describes the process by which people gain the right to vote. The correct answer is ENFRANCHISED (Word 246).

6. E

The question asks you to find a word that describes a pivotal or turning point event. The correct answer is WATERSHED (Word 242).

7. E

The question asks you to find a first word that means "very greedy" and a second word that means "generosity." The key word "antithesis" or opposite signals that the answer will be a pair of antonyms. The correct answer is AVARICE (Word 229) and MUNIFICENT (Word 232).

8. C

The question asks you to find a word that describes the misappropriation of funds. The correct answer is MALFEASANCE (Word 260).

9. E

The question asks you to find a first word that would have a negative impact upon the second word. The second word must be consistent with an organization that has an "open and non-hierarchical structure." The correct answers are AUTOCRATIC (Word 244) and EGALITARIAN (Word 248) because Getlein's AUTOCRATIC leanings would mean that he would want more and more power and would thus "undermine" the company's EGALITARIAN culture.

10. A

The question asks you to find a word describing an "infectious" disease that quickly spread "throughout the entire country." The correct answer is VIRULENT (Word 221).

Chapter 8

WORDS WITH MULTIPLE MEANINGS: 261–280

Learning new vocabulary words is a challenge when a word has a single meaning. Many students are surprised to discover that there are words that have multiple meanings. For example, everyone knows that a flag is a rectangular piece of fabric with a distinctive design that is used to symbolize a nation. But FLAG can also mean to lose energy or interest.

SAT test writers have long been aware of words with multiple meanings. Since students think they know what these words mean, they often eliminate the word and miss the question. In fact, words like FLAG are among the most-missed words on the SAT.

This chapter will examine and illustrate 20 commonly-used words with multiple meanings. Our focus will be on these words' secondary definitions, the ones SAT test writers use to test your knowledge. So be prepared to learn that everyday words like CHECK, COIN, and even PEDESTRIAN have less commonly-used secondary meanings.

261. ARREST:
To bring to a stop; halt

What is the first thing you think of when you hear the word ARREST? For most, ARREST probably calls to mind a police officer and handcuffs. ARREST does mean to seize and hold under the authority of the law.

It is important to know that the word ARREST has other meanings. SAT test writers will use ARREST to mean to bring to a stop or halt. Environmentalists, for example, hope to ARREST the growth of carbon dioxide emissions in the earth's atmosphere. One way to remember this use of ARREST is to think of a cardiac ARREST. This condition takes place when there is an abrupt stoppage of normal blood circulation due to heart failure.

262. GRAVITY:
A serious situation or problem

Everyone has heard the expression, "Whatever goes up, must come down." This saying is true due to the law of GRAVITY. In physics, GRAVITY refers to the natural force of attraction exerted by a celestial body.

On October 22, 1962, President Kennedy informed a stunned nation that the Soviet Union had SURREPTITIOUSLY (Word 17) placed intermediate-range nuclear missiles in Cuba. The President underscored the GRAVITY of the crisis when he ordered a naval blockade of Cuba and sternly warned that the United States would react to any missile launched from Cuba with a "full retaliatory response upon the Soviet Union."

263. PRECIPITATE:
A result or outcome of an action

Most people associate the word PRECIPITATION with rain, snow, or sleet. However, PRECIPITATE can also refer to a result or outcome of an action. Test writers often use PRECIPITATE on AP US History questions. For example, the discovery of Soviet missiles in Cuba PRECIPITATED the Cuban Missile Crisis.

264. RELIEF:
Elevation of a land surface

What is the first thing that comes to your mind when you hear the word RELIEF? In everyday usage, RELIEF most commonly refers to the feeling of ease when a burden has been removed or lightened. For example, in baseball a RELIEF pitcher eases the burden of the starting pitcher. However, RELIEF can also be used as a geographic term that refers to the elevation of a land surface. For example, RELIEF maps of the United States rise at the Appalachian Mountains in the East and at the Rocky Mountains in the West.

265. CHECK:
To restrain; halt; hold back; contain

We are all familiar with the word CHECK. We earn CHECKS, cash CHECKS, and CHECK our work on math problems. Airline passengers check in at the ticket counter and hotel guests CHECK in at the registration counter. SAT test writers know that you are familiar with these everyday uses of the word CHECK. It is important to remember that the word CHECK can also mean to restrain, halt, or hold back. For example, our Constitution calls for a system of

CHECKS and balances to restrain each branch of government. During the Cold War, the U.S. policy of containment was designed to CHECK the expansion of Soviet power and influence. And hockey fans know that a CHECK is when one player blocks or impedes the movement of an opponent.

266. FLAG:
To become weak, feeble, or spiritless; to lose interest

Like CHECK (Word 265), FLAG is a familiar word. For most people, a flag is a banner or emblem used to symbolize a country, state, or community. FLAG, however, can also mean to become weak or to lose interest. Whenever the singer Beyoncé wins an award, for example, she always thanks her parents for keeping her spirits up and never letting her enthusiasm FLAG. She says that her parents keep her motivation strong and her mind focused.

267. DISCRIMINATING:
Characterized by the ability to make fine distinctions; refined taste

Is DISCRIMINATING a negative or a positive word? Actually, it can be both. Most people consider DISCRIMINATING a negative word because it refers to the act of treating a person, racial group, or minority unfairly. Surprisingly, DISCRIMINATING can be a positive word when it refers to someone's ability to make fine distinctions and thus demonstrate good taste. For example, CONNOISSEURS (knowledgeable amateurs) are known for their DISCRIMINATING taste in rare wine, fine clothes, and valuable art. In the

James Bond movies, Bond is a secret agent who displays DISCRIMINATING taste by ordering vodka martinis ("shaken, not stirred"), wearing Omega watches and wearing stylish tuxedos.

268. ECLIPSE:
Overshadow; outshine; surpass

In astronomy, an ECLIPSE is the total or partial covering of one celestial body by another. A solar ECLIPSE, for example, occurs when the moon passes between the sun and the earth. ECLIPSE, however, can also be a verb meaning to overshadow or surpass. Taylor Hicks, for instance, won the fifth season of *American Idol*. The fourth place finisher, Chris Daughtry, nonetheless ECLIPSED Hicks in both popularity and record sales. A similar pattern can be seen in IndyCar racing. Scott Dixon won the 2008 Indianapolis 500. Although she didn't finish the race, Danica Patrick has ECLIPSED Dixon in both media attention and endorsements.

269. COIN:
To devise a new word or phrase

If you see the word COIN in a PSAT or SAT question, the first image that will probably come to your mind will be the image of a penny, nickel, dime, or quarter. While COIN is most commonly used to refer to a small piece of money, it can also mean to create a new word or phrase. The English language is not static. New words are COINED or created all the time. For example, Janine Benyus is a natural sciences writer who COINED the word "biomimicry" to describe the art of copying nature's biological principles of design.

Ms. Benyus COINED the term by combining the Greek "bios," meaning "life," and "mimesis," meaning "imitate." For example, architects in London are using biomimetic principles derived from ocean sponges to design buildings that are far more energy-efficient.

270. STOCK:

A stereotypical and formulaic character in a novel or film

The word STOCK has 13 different definitions ranging from the merchandise in a store to a unit of ownership in a company. While SAT test writers are aware of these different definitions, they are most interested in STOCK as a literary term referring to formulaic characters. Teen movies such as *Clueless, Mean Girls,* and *Superbad* all feature STOCK characters such as "The Perfect Girl," "The Blonde Bimbo," "The Popular Jock," and "The Awkward BUT Ultimately Beautiful Girl." These STOCK characters are easily recognizable but one-dimensional and TRITE (Word 36).

271. CURRENCY:

General acceptance or use, prevalence

What is the first thought that comes to your mind when you hear the word CURRENCY? Most people probably immediately think of money. However, SAT test writers are not most people. They know that CURRENCY can also mean an idea that is becoming widespread or prevalent. For example, in his book *Quiet Strength*, Tony Dungy argues that a coach should treat his or her players with respect and avoid screaming at them. When he was Head Coach of the Indianapolis Colts, Dungy practiced what he preached. Although Dungy's view is gaining CURRENCY, many coaches still rely on old-fashioned TIRADES (Word 100) to motivate their players.

272. BENT:
A strong tendency; a leaning; an inclination

Have you ever said, "This nail is BENT; I can't use it?" For most people, the word BENT means twisted. However, BENT can also mean a strong tendency or disposition to follow a particular course of action. For example, the world-famous artist Pablo Picasso demonstrated a BENT toward drawing from an early age. According to his family, Picasso's BENT was so great that he drew pictures before he could talk!

While Picasso's artistic BENT guided him to create works of art, the Joker's (*The Dark Knight*) MAL-EVOLENT (malicious) BENT led him to create chaos and destruction. Because he is BENT on destruction for destruction's sake, the Joker is Batman's most formidable and IMPLACABLE (Word 182) foe.

273. COURT:
To attempt to gain the favor or support of a person or group

Most people associate the word COURT with a place. For example, a COURT is where people play tennis or basketball. A COURT is also a place where justice is administered by a judge or a jury. But, COURT can also be used as a verb. For example, when politicians run for office, they COURT votes. During the early 1970s, Richard Nixon COURTED the "Silent Major-ity," a group of voters who supported his Vietnam War policies and opposed the counterculture. In the 1980s,

Ronald Reagan COURTED "Reagan Democrats," blue-collar workers who traditionally supported the Democratic Party. Today, candidates from both parties are working hard to COURT young voters.

274. NEGOTIATE:
To successfully travel through, around, or over an obstacle or terrain

The word NEGOTIATE is very familiar to students studying American history. Our national history is filled with examples of diplomats NEGOTIATING treaties and labor leaders NEGOTIATING contracts. But the word NEGOTIATE can also mean to successfully travel through, around, or over an obstacle or difficult terrain. For example, settlers traveling along the Oregon Trail had to NEGOTIATE their way across broad streams and over steep mountain passes. In the *Lord of the Rings* trilogy, Frodo, Bilbo, and Samwise had to NEGOTIATE a series of formidable obstacles before reaching the Crack of Doom in Mordor.

275. TEMPER:
To soften; moderate; MITIGATE (Word 31)

TEMPER is a word with contradictory meanings. On the one hand, TEMPER refers to a sudden burst of anger. On the other hand, TEMPER means to soften or moderate one's emotions. In the movie *Happy Gilmore*, Happy illustrates both meanings of TEMPER. Happy loses his TEMPER on the golf course as he fights with Bob Barker and almost comes to blows with Shooter McGavin. Virginia successfully persuades Happy that he must TEMPER his anger. As a result, Happy defeats Shooter, wins over Virginia, and saves his grandmother's home.

276. PEDESTRIAN:

Undistinguished; ordinary; conventional

How can the word PEDESTRIAN have to do with both crosswalks and graduation speakers? PEDESTRIANS, or people who travel on foot, should use specially-designed crosswalks to cross busy highways. On the other hand, graduation speakers should avoid PEDESTRIAN statements such as "we begin a new chapter in our lives" or "this is not the end but the beginning." Why do we call these age-old clichés PEDESTRIAN? That's because the word PEDES-TRIAN can also mean ordinary and conventional. Needless to say, this is the meaning that you will encounter on your SAT!

 Tip for a Direct Hit

The Latin word *ped* means "foot." An IMPEDIMENT is something that gets in the way of your feet and thus interferes with progress. In contrast, EXPEDITE means to remove (*ex* = out) obstacles that get in the way of your feet and thus to speed up a process. That's why EXPEDITED service is supposed to be faster than regular service.

277. CAVALIER:

An arrogant attitude; a haughty disregard for others

Fans of NBA basketball teams and University of Virginia athletic teams will quickly recognize the word

CAVALIER as the nickname of the Cleveland Cavaliers and the UVA Cavaliers. The nickname makes sense. During the Middle Ages a CAVALIER was a gallant or chivalrous man. Would this knowledge help you on the SAT? Unfortunately, it might mislead you. CAVALIER also describes an arrogant and haughty disregard for others. The CAVALIER statement "Let them eat cake" is commonly attributed to the French queen, Marie Antoinette. She supposedly made this CAVALIER remark upon hearing that the French people had no bread to eat. Her CAVALIER attitude inflamed popular ANTAGONISM (great dislike) toward her and may have contributed to her trip to the guillotine. Today, a CAVALIER attitude won't cost you your head, but it could cost you friends and popularity.

278. SANCTION:
An official approval/disproval for an action

SANCTION is one of the few words in the English language that has diametrically opposite meanings. When it is used in a positive sense, SANCTION means official approval or permission. For example, if your school district SANCTIONS cell phones, then you have permission to bring them to school. But, when SANCTION is used in a negative sense, it means official disapproval and thus the risk of incurring penalties. If your school district SANCTIONS against cell phone use, you don't have permission to bring them to school. It is important to note that College Board rules impose strict SANCTIONS on students who forget to turn off cell phones off during the SAT.

279. COMPROMISE:

To reduce the quality or value of something; to jeopardize or place at risk

American history is filled with famous compromises in which two sides settled their differences by making concessions. This use of the word COMPROMISE is so common that it is easy to forget that COMPROMISE can also mean to jeopardize the quality or value of something. For example, identify theft has COMPROMISED the personal information of millions of Americans. The quality of a product can be COMPROMISED by inferior materials. And finally, it is also possible for a cultural value to be COMPROMISED. Many PUNDITS (Word 117) believe that the values of hard work, patience, and diligence are being COMPROMISED by our culture's PENCHANT (Word 62) for instant gratification.

280. CHANNEL:

To direct or guide along a desired course

Why would the word CHANNEL appear on the SAT? Everyone knows that a CHANNEL has to do with radio and television stations. But CHANNEL can also mean to direct or guide along a desired course. For example, in the movie *Iron Man*, Tony Stark is a billionaire industrialist and genius inventor who spends most of his time being a carefree playboy. His life suddenly changed when terrorists kidnapped Tony and ordered him to build a devastating weapon. Instead, Tony CHANNELED his creative energies into building a high-tech suit of armor that enabled him to escape. Upon returning to America, Tony refined his armor and CHANNELED his energies into protecting the world as the invincible Iron Man!

Testing Your Vocabulary

Each SAT contains 19 sentence completion questions that are primarily a test of your vocabulary. Each sentence completion will always have a key word or phrase that will lead you to the correct answer. Use the vocabulary from Chapters 6-8 to circle the answer to each of the following 10 sentence completion questions. You'll find answers and explanations on pages 66-68.

1. John Dean's accusations that top White House officials obstructed justice by trying to cover up the Watergate break-in _____ a sequence of events that led to President Nixon's resignation.

    (A) negotiated
    (B) precipitated
    (C) arrested
    (D) eclipsed
    (E) tempered

2. Determined to reduce global carbon dioxide emissions, leading environmentalists called for international _____ that _____ the growth of inefficient coal-burning factories.

    (A) paradigms .. foster
    (B) accords .. arrest
    (C) manifestos .. reaffirm
    (D) mandates .. encourage
    (E) anecdotes .. combat

3. The park guide warned the novice hikers to avoid advanced trails that contained rugged natural obstacles and were therefore difficult to _____.

    (A) court
    (B) eclipse
    (C) nullify
    (D) enfranchise
    (E) negotiate

4. Because they were based upon rigorously collected _____ data and not abstract theories, Professor Halle's revolutionary conclusions _____ all previous studies by making them obsolete.

    (A) experimental .. reinforced
    (B) stock .. surpassed
    (C) questionable .. strengthened
    (D) secondhand .. obliterated
    (E) empirical .. eclipsed

5. The once upbeat candidate had to _____ her initial optimism as new polling data indicated that her popular support had begun to significantly erode.

    (A) temper
    (B) coerce
    (C) intensify
    (D) exonerate
    (E) remunerate

6. Rapper Ludacris' name is actually an amalgam: he combined his given name Chris with the first part of the word ludicrous to _____ his popular stage name.

   (A) check
   (B) court
   (C) precipitate
   (D) coin
   (E) enlighten

7. Located in Australia, Uluru or Ayers Rock is an ancient sandstone formation that is often called an "island mountain" because it provides the only natural _____ in an otherwise flat and barren plain.

   (A) relief
   (B) bent
   (C) watershed
   (D) archipelago
   (E) paradigm

8. Americans understood the full _____ of the Cuban Missile Crisis when President Kennedy, calmly but with great seriousness, informed the public that any attack on the United States from Cuba would trigger a full nuclear retaliation against the Soviet Union.

   (A) currency
   (B) extravagance
   (C) virulence
   (D) gravity
   (E) avarice

9. Critics panned the new action adventure film, saying that it was a trite story filled with _____ characters who were both formulaic and stereotypical.

    (A) munificent
    (B) unprecedented
    (C) stock
    (D) anecdotal
    (E) ironic

10. Selective taste and _____ judgment are essential for buying Modernist paintings, since a mistake can have expensive consequences.

    (A) belligerent
    (B) extravagant
    (C) crystallized
    (D) caustic
    (E) discriminating

Answers and Explanations

1. **B**

    The question asks you to find a word describing the impact of John Dean's accusations. The correct answer is PRECIPITATED (Word 263) since Dean's accusations led to President Nixon's resignation.

2. **B**

    The question asks you to find two logically connected actions that environmentalists committed to reducing global carbon dioxide emissions would advocate. The correct answer is ACCORDS (Word 236) and ARREST (Word 261). In other words, environmentalists want international agreements to halt the growth of carbon-burning factories.

3. **E**

    The question asks you to find a word describing the effect "rugged natural obstacles" would have on an advanced trail. The correct answer is NEGOTIATE (Word 274) since these obstacles would make the trail difficult to hike.

4. **E**

    The question asks you to find a first word that means "rigorously collected" and is the opposite of "abstract theories." The correct answer to the first blank is therefore EMPIRICAL (Word 222). The question then asks you to find a second word describing the impact Halle's EMPIR-ICALLY-based revolutionary conclusions would have upon the previous theoretical studies. The correct answer to the second blank is ECLIPSED (Word 268) since the new EMPIRICAL data made all previous studies "obsolete."

5. **A**

The question asks you to find a word describing the impact the "new polling data" would have upon the "once-upbeat" candidate. The correct answer is TEMPER (WORD 275) since her falling popular support would force the candidate to TEMPER or moderate her "initial optimism."

6. **D**

The question asks you to find a word describing the creation of a new name or word. The correct answer is COIN (Word 269) since Ludacris is a coined or newly-devised name.

7. **A**

The question asks you to find a word describing an "island mountain" on "an otherwise flat plain." The correct answer is RELIEF (Word 264) since Uluru or Ayers Rock is an elevated landform on a flat plain.

8. **D**

The question asks you to find a word that is consistent with President Kennedy's "great seriousness." The correct answer is GRAVITY (Word 262).

9. C

The question asks you to find a word describing characters who "were both formulaic and stereotyped." The correct answer is STOCK (Word 270).

10. E

The question asks you to find a word that is consistent with "selective taste" and logically essential to avoid making a mistake with "expensive consequences." The correct answer is DISCRIMINATING (Word 267).

Chapter 9

THE TOUGHEST WORDS I: 281–340

Do you know what the words DILATORY, CAPITULATE, and BURGEON mean? If so, congratulations! You have an excellent vocabulary. If not, don't be upset. These words are all answers or answer choices to Level 5 questions, the toughest ones on the SAT. Only about 20 percent of students correctly answer a Level 5 question.

Paradoxically, Level 5 questions are both the toughest and the easiest on the SAT. They are tough because the word choices deliberately include challenging words known to only a small percentage of students. They are easy because, if you know the words, the clues are often very straightforward and lead directly to the correct answer.

Chapters 9 and 10 focus on 120 Level 5 vocabulary words. Each of these words was the answer to a very difficult question on recent SATs. Knowing the meanings of these words will significantly raise your SAT score by helping you infuse great vocabulary into your essay, understand difficult critical reading passages, and master challenging sentence completion questions. As always, we have worked hard to find vivid examples to illustrate each word. Don't be DILATORY (late). There is no reason to CAPITULATE (surrender). Study these words and you will experience the pleasure of having a BURGEONING (rapidly expanding) vocabulary and a rising SAT score!

281. LAMBASTE:
Denounce; strongly criticize

Movie critics EFFUSIVELY (Word 36) praised the film *Avatar* for its cutting-edge digital special effects. However, the same critics LAMBASTED the movie for its PEDESTRIAN (Word 276) plot and PLATITUDE-filled (Word 36) dialogue. One critic wrote that *Avatar* is "a world to behold and a story to forget."

282. QUIESCENT:
Marked by inactivity; a state of quiet repose

In CE 79, Pompeii was a prosperous Roman town of ten to 20 thousand people. Pompeians planted vineyards and grazed their sheep on the slopes of nearby Mt. Vesuvius. The mountain appeared to be benign and QUIESCENT, but looks were deceiving. On August 24, CE 79, Mt. Vesuvius erupted, transforming Pompeii from a lively, crowded city into a ghost town. Modern geologists now know that Mt. Vesuvius is far from QUIESCENT. It is one of the most potentially dangerous volcanoes in the world because of the three million people who live close to it.

283. PROVISIONAL:
Tentative; temporary; for the time being (like a PROVISIONAL driver's license)

Quick: how many planets are there in the Solar System? If you answered nine you were right up until 2006. From the time of its discovery in 1930 until 2006, Pluto was counted as the Solar System's ninth planet. However, this classification proved to be PROVISIONAL. On August 24, 2006, the International Astronomical Union (IAU) reclassified Pluto as a member of a new category of dwarf planets. So now the Solar System contains eight official planets and at least three dwarf planets, including Pluto. Pluto's PROVISIONAL status has raised a storm of controversy. Insisting that Pluto should still be a planet, traditionalists have protested the IAU's decision. The controversy has resulted in the COINING (Word 269) of a new verb "plutoed." Chosen as the 2006 Word of the Year, "to Pluto" means to demote or devalue someone or something.

284. LURID:
Sensational; shocking; ghastly

During the late 1890s, newspaper publishers, led by William Randolph Hearst and Joseph Pulitzer, attempted to outdo each other with sensational headlines and LURID stories about alleged atrocities in Cuba. For example, Hearst's *Journal American* published a LURID sketch depicting Spanish officials disrobing and searching an American woman.

285. TRUCULENT, PUGNACIOUS, BELLIGERENT:
Defiantly aggressive; eager to fight

On February 15, 1898, the battleship *Maine* mysteriously blew up, causing the loss of 200 sailors in Havana harbor. Led by Theodore Roosevelt, TRUCULENT Americans demanded that President McKinley call for a declaration of war. When the cautious president delayed, the PUGNACIOUS Roosevelt reportedly snarled that McKinley had "The backbone of a chocolate éclair." TR's BELLIGERENT attitude left no LATITUDE (leeway) for compromise.

286. PROPITIATE:

To appease; to conciliate; to regain the favor or goodwill of

Stung by Roosevelt's barb (see Word 285) and shaken by the public's demand for revenge, President McKinley recognized the inevitable and PROPITIATED both Roosevelt and the public. On April 11, 1898, McKinley sent a war message to Congress urging armed intervention to avenge the sinking of the *Maine* and to free oppressed Cubans.

287. ÉLAN:

A vigorous spirit; a great enthusiasm

A leader of unbounded energy, Theodore Roosevelt promptly formed a volunteer regiment nicknamed the "Rough Riders" to spearhead the American invasion of Cuba. The Rough Riders included a mixture of cowboys, Ivy League graduates, and star athletes. Although short on discipline, the Rough Riders were long on ÉLAN. Dressed in a uniform custom-made by Brooks Brothers, TR demonstrated both courage and ÉLAN as he led a victorious charge up San Juan Hill.

288. PERFUNCTORY:

Something performed in a spiritless, mechanical, and routine manner

In her rendition of Rudy Clark's "Shoop Shoop Song (It's In His Kiss)," Cher famously poses this question: "Does he love me, I wanna know, how can I tell if he loves me so?" Cher provides the following answer: "If you wanna know if he loves you so, it's in his kiss, that's where it is." So what is the difference between a passionate kiss that proves he loves you and a PERF-

UNCTORY kiss that suggests he doesn't? A passionate kiss is filled with emotion and feeling. In contrast, a PERFUNCTORY kiss is a quick routine peck on the cheek. A PERFUNCTORY kiss probably means that a relationship is becoming routine and lacks passion.

289. APLOMB:
Self-assurance; confident composure; admirable poise under pressure

On March 4, 1933, over 100,000 Americans gathered around the Capitol building to hear Franklin D. Roosevelt's Inaugural Address. The national mood was as bleak as the grey clouds on that cold Saturday. Faced with plummeting unemployment, falling stock prices and collapsing banks, the government seemed paralyzed. But FDR was UNDAUNTED (Word 73). With his confident and characteristic APLOMB, Roosevelt proclaimed that "The only thing we have to fear is fear itself." The President's APLOMB lifted the nation's spirit. Witnesses reported that at the end of FDR's speech, the applause was thunderous, rolling like waves across Washington D.C.

290. OPACITY:
Hard to understand; impenetrably dense and obscure

Read the sentence reprinted below and on the next page describing a painting entitled *October* by the modern American artist Kenneth Noland:

"The prototypical Circles, numbering some 175 examples, alone embrace a multitude of moods and means – from propulsive versus sun-drenched hues to those of the type of October,

displaying an economy, coolness, and quiddity that almost anticipate a Minimalist aesthetic."

Do you understand what the author is trying to say? Is the writer LUCID (clear) or OPAQUE? If you were an editor, would you keep or revise the sentence? Most editors would probably revise or delete this dense sentence because its OPACITY makes it incomprehensible for all but the most knowledgeable readers.

291. CRAVEN:
Characterized by acting in a cowardly manner

What do Fredo Corleone (*The Godfather*) and the Cowardly Lion (*Wizard of Oz*) have in common? Both were known for their CRAVEN behavior. The FECKLESS (weak and irresponsible) Fredo was assigned unimportant family jobs. As everyone knows, the Cowardly Lion behaved in a CRAVEN manner because he lacked courage.

292. VENAL:
Corrupt, dishonest, open to bribery

In the movie *300*, what do the Ephors, Ephialtes, and Theron all have in common? They are all VENAL traitors who accepted bribes from Xerxes to betray Sparta. The VENAL Ephors accepted bribes to reject King Leonidas's plan to repel the Persians. The VENAL Ephialtes accepted bribes to reveal the location of a secret path around the Spartan position at Thermopylae. And the VENAL Theron accepted bribes to betray Queen Gorgo. The Spartans ultimately triumphed over these VENAL traitors. Leonidas and his heroic 300 Spartan warriors gave up their lives to delay the Persian advance. Queen Gorgo killed the Theron, revealing a bag of Persian coins hidden in his cloak. Outraged and now aware that they had been betrayed, the Spartan army defeated the Persians at the Battle of Plataea.

293. LICENTIOUS:
Immoral; DISSOLUTE; debauched

In his book *The Twelve Caesars*, the Roman historian Suetonious described the LICENTIOUS behavior of the first Roman emperors. He particularly DECRIED (Word 174) the DISSOLUTE antics of Emperor Caligula. When Caligula's grandmother Antonia ADMONISHED (Word 69) him to change his ways, Caligula rebuked her with the remark, "Remember that I have the right to do anything to anybody." Drunk with power, Caligula bathed in perfume, built great pleasure barges, and demanded that he be worshipped as a god. Caligula's LICENTIOUS reign came to an abrupt end when one of his guards killed him in a secret passage of the palace. At first, many Romans hesitated to believe the news, fearing that this was a trick of the DISSOLUTE emperor to discover who would rejoice at his death.

294. NOXIOUS:
Harmful; injurious to physical, mental or moral health

China's lax environmental policies and repressive political system is NOXIOUS to its citizens' physical and moral well-being. Every night, columns of freight trucks spewing dark clouds of diesel exhaust rumble into China's crowded cities. These NOXIOUS fumes are by far China's largest source of street-level pollution. Meanwhile, China is a NOXIOUS one-party state where thousands of its citizens are imprisoned for "crimes" ranging from advocating a multiparty system to using the Internet to call for governmental reform.

295. SUPERFLUOUS and EXTRANEOUS:
Unnecessary; extra

The movie *The Dark Knight* includes scenes in which Batman leaves Gotham City and travels to Hong Kong. This marks the first time that Batman has ever left Gotham. While some critics and fans praised this UNPRECEDENTED (Word 259) dramatic development, others criticized it as a SUPERFLUOUS SUBPLOT (Word 211). For example, one movie critic called it a "pointless jaunt" in an otherwise brilliant movie. What is your opinion? Do you think the Hong Kong scenes were essential to the story or EXTRANEOUS scenes that should have been deleted?

296. DUPLICITOUS:
Deliberately deceptive in behavior or speech

What do Ferris Bueller (*Ferris Bueller's Day Off*), Dewey Finn (*School of Rock*), and Frank Abagnale Jr. (*Catch Me if You Can*) have in common? All three were DUPLICITOUS, but all three lied with great PANACHE (Word 81) or flair. Ferris dined at an expensive restaurant while pretending to be Abe Fromer, a Chicago sausage king. Dewey impersonated Ned so that he could take a job as a substitute teacher at a prestigious elementary school. And the 18-year-old Frank convinced Brenda that he was a Harvard graduate, a doctor, and a Lutheran.

297. PROFLIGATE:

Wasteful; someone who SQUANDERS (wastes) time and money by living for the moment

Hollywood stars tend to be more PROFLIGATE than PARSIMONIOUS (Word 233). Tom and Katie Cruise's motto seems to be "Spend, spend, spend." Tom owns four private jets, including a $28 million Gulfstream. The Cruises annually spend over $1 million just on fuel for their jaunts around the world. The PROFLIGATE couple spared no expense on their daughter's second birthday party. They filled a rented Hollywood Hills mansion with $17,000 worth of flowers and spent $45,000 on food. Yellow and white sugar butterflies adorned Suri's $5,000 four-tier birthday cake. The PROFLIGATE and EXORBITANT (Word 162) party cost an estimated $100,000.

298. EPIPHANY:

A sudden realization; an insightful moment

Have you ever performed in a school play? For most students, acting in a school play is a great way to meet people and have fun. But for a few student-actors, it can be a life-changing experience. For example, when Leighton Meester was just 11, she performed in her school play *The Wizard of Oz*. As she was performing, Leighton had an EPIPHANY: "I realized acting was what I wanted to do." Leighton turned her EPIPHANY into reality. Today she plays Blair Waldorf in the popular television program *Gossip Girl*.

299. INSIDIOUS:
Causing harm in a subtle or stealthy manner; devious

In *The Scarlet Letter*, Roger Chillingworth is Hester Prynne's long-absent husband. He returns to Boston only to find that Hester has had an affair with an unknown man and is now the mother of an illegitimate daughter. Consumed with revenge, Chillingworth vows to find and then psychologically torture Hester's secret lover. Sensing a hidden guilt, Chillingworth soon launches an INSIDIOUS plan to torment the Reverend Arthur Dimmesdale.

300. VACUOUS and INANE:
Empty; lacking serious purpose; VAPID

On the TV show *Glee*, Brittany is a VACUOUS cheerleader who is prone to making INANE comments. For example, Brittany responded to Mr. Schuster's question "Does anyone know what a ballad is?" by answering, "A male duck." But no one could accuse Brittany of creating the "Glist List" of school hotties because as she admitted, "I don't know how to turn on a computer."

301. HARBINGER, PORTENT, PRESAGE:
Indications or omens that something important or calamitous is about to occur

Recent scientific studies have confirmed that the North Pole is melting. This startling fact PRESAGES difficult times for polar bears and other Arctic animals that rely on sea ice to survive. It is also a HARBINGER of coming trouble for humans. The melting ice will raise sea levels, thus posing a threat to coastal cities and villages. Alarmed scientists are warning world leaders that these PORTENTS should not be ignored. They are calling for international ACCORDS (Word 236) to ARREST (Word 261) the growth of carbon dioxide emissions.

302. BELEAGUER:
To beset; to surround with problems

In the movie *Remember the Titans*, Herman Boone, a successful black football coach from North Carolina, is hired to replace the popular white coach Bill Yoast at newly integrated T.C. Williams High School in Alexandria, Virginia. Boone is immediately BELEAG-UERED by a host of problems. Outraged by his demotion, Yoast threatens to resign. At the same time, tensions quickly erupt between black and white members of the football team. These tensions reflect the turmoil in Alexandria, where extremists resent Coach Boone and demand that he resign.

303. BURGEON:
To grow rapidly and expand

Although BELEAGUERED (see Word 302) by seemingly INSURMOUNTABLE (Word 185) problems, Coach Boone proved to be RESOLUTE (Word 330) and resourceful. He ADROITLY (Word 67) unified both his coaching staff and his team. Once they learned to work together, the Titans won victory after victory. Community support soon BURGEONED as the town and school rallied behind their victorious and unified football team.

304. IMPERIOUS:
Domineering and arrogant; haughty

What do the Persian ruler Xerxes, the English King Henry VIII, and the French king Louis XIV have in common? All three were IMPERIOUS leaders. Xerxes IMPERIOUSLY insisted that his subjects all bow down before their god-king. Henry VIII IMPERIOUSLY demanded obedience from both his subjects and his wives. Louis XIV IMPERIOUSLY (but truthfully) explained that in France, "L'État, c'est moi," meaning "The State is me."

305. PETULANT:
Peevish, irritable

Britney Spears is notorious for her PETULANT behavior. For example, just an hour before going on stage at the MTV Video Music Awards, Britney PETULANTLY insisted on doing her own hair. She abruptly told her hair stylist, "You're really annoying me. Get out!" The PETULANT Pop Princess ended up doing her own hair, which proved to be a FIASCO (Word 146).

306. COMPLAISANT:
Amiable; agreeable; marked by a pleasing personality; AFFABLE (Word 18)

Compare Britney Spears with Giselle, the fairy tale princess, in the movie *Enchanted*. While Britney is PETULANT (Word 305) and peevish, Giselle exudes a natural goodness that delights both humans and animals. Her COMPLAISANT personality even charms notoriously ill-tempered New Yorkers who stop what they are doing to spontaneously sing and dance with the ever-AFFABLE (Word 18) Giselle.

Tip for a Direct Hit

It is important to note that although COMPLAISANT and complacent sound alike, they are two very different words. Complacent means over-contented and self-satisfied. In contrast, COMPLAISANT is derived from the prefix *com*, meaning "with," and the root *plaisir*, meaning "pleasure." So COMPLAISANT literally means "with pleasure" and thus demonstrating a pleasing personality.

307. FAWN:

To behave in a servile manner; SUBSERVIENT

In *300*, Xerxes promises Leonidas great wealth and power. All the Spartan king has to do is kneel before the Persian god-king. But Leonidas is a proud Spartan who refuses to act in a FAWNING manner toward anyone. Leonidas rebuffs Xerxes, saying, "Kneeling will be hard for me. I'm afraid killing all those slaves of yours has left me with a nasty cramp in my leg."

308. OBDURATE and INTRANSIGIENT:

Very stubborn; obstinate; unyieldingly persistent; inflexible; INTRACTABLE

What do the Spartan leader King Leonidas and President Woodrow Wilson have in common? They were both very OBDURATE. In the movie *300*, Leonidas OBDURATELY insisted that "The battle is over when I say it is over. No surrender. No retreat." Similarly, Wilson OBDURATELY refused to accept any of Senator Lodge's reservations that would modify the League of Nations. The INTRANSIGIENT Wilson insisted, "I shall consent to nothing."

309. REDOLENT:
Exuding fragrance; full of a specified smell

In her Harry Potter series, author J.K. Rowling often describes how the REDOLENT fragrance of a particularly delicious feast would WAFT (float) across the Great Hall at Hogwarts. In Faulkner's novels, the REDOLENT fragrance of magnolia blooms seems almost to WAFT from the book's pages.

310. CHICANERY:
Deception by subterfuge; deliberate trickery

In her book, *Century of Dishonor*, Helen Hunt Jackson exposed the American government's CHICANERY in deliberately cheating the Native Americans. For example, Jackson sharply criticized government officials for their CHICANERY in signing treaties they had no intention of honoring. In the movie *Iron Man*, Pepper Potts exposed Obadiah Stane's CHICANERY in deliberately selling weapons to both the U.S. troops and the Ten Rings terrorists. Stane's CHICANERY did not end with supplying weapons to American's enemies. Potts discovered that Stane also hired the terrorists to kill his business partner, Tony Stark.

311. CONUNDRUM:
A difficult problem; a dilemma with no easy solution

In the movie *Knocked Up*, slacker Ben Stone and ambitious, career-minded Allison Scott meet at a local night club and then spend the night together. The following morning, they quickly discover that they have little in common. Eight weeks later, Allison is shocked to discover that she is pregnant. She then contacts the equally-shocked Ben to tell him the news. Allison and Ben now face a difficult CONUNDRUM. Will Allison choose to be a single mother or will she and Ben give their relationship a chance?

312. SLIGHT:
A disrespectful or disparaging remark

In Volume 1, Grand Master Larry DEBUNKED (Word 178) Kanye West. Now it's Lindsay Lohan's turn to take GML's razor-sharp SLIGHTS, SAGE (wise) advice, and PERTINENT (Word 254) questions:

> *Yo Lindsay you're easy to SLIGHT,*
> *Cause we're not tight.*
> *I don't want to frighten,*
> *I'm here to ENLIGHTEN (Word 237).*

> *Once your fans were ELATED (very happy),*
> *Movies like Mean Girls were gold-plated.*
> *Now they rejoice,*
> *When your movie is not a choice.*

> *Being BOORISH (Word 64) is not refined,*
> *The way to success is clearly defined.*
> *Don't be so dumb,*
> *Act with more APLOMB (Word 289).*

> *It's time to take STOCK(Word 270),*
> *Can you still rock?*
> *Maybe you should study the DH vocab,*
> *While you have the time in rehab.*

313. CAPITULATE:
To surrender; comply without protest

What do the King Leonidas and General George Washington have in common? Both refused to CAPITULATE when faced with certain defeat. In the movie *300*, King Leonidas refused to CAPITULATE to the Persians when he defiantly insisted, "Spartans never surrender. Spartans never retreat." Similarly, George Washington refused to CAPITULATE when the British and Hessians had apparently trapped his army on the Pennsylvania side of the Delaware River. Defiantly telling his troops, "Victory or Death!", Washington boldly crossed the ice-filled Delaware on Christmas Eve and surprised the Hessians at Trenton.

314. DISHEARTENING:
Very discouraging; dismaying; dispiriting

What do Samuel Tilden and Al Gore have in common? Both men were Democratic presidential candidates who won the popular vote but suffered DISHEARTENING defeats in the Electoral College. Tilden lost the controversial 1876 election and Gore lost the hotly disputed 2000 election. However, both men overcame their DISHEARTENING defeats. Tilden became a major benefactor of the New York Public Library, and Gore has become one of the world's foremost environmental activists.

315. APOCRYPHAL:
Of doubtful authenticity

American students have long been taught that the Spanish explorer Ponce de Leon discovered Florida while searching for the Fountain of Youth. The story is

APOCRYPHAL. While Ponce de Leon did discover Florida, there is no evidence that he was searching for the Fountain of Youth. Like other Spanish conquistadores, he was searching for gold and new lands to expand the Spanish Empire.

316. MAGISTERIAL:
Learned and authoritative

In England, a magistrate was a royal official entrusted with the administration of the laws. Magistrates naturally wanted to appear MAGISTERIAL or learned and authoritative. In the movie *The Wizard of Oz*, the Munchkin mayor wanted to appear MAGISTERIAL when he grandly welcomed Dorothy by publicly proclaiming, "As Mayor of the Munchkin City in the County of the Land of Oz, I welcome you most regally." The Mayor's MAGISTERIAL tone continued when he announced that the Wicked Witch is "Positively, absolutely, undeniably, and reliably dead."

317. PLASTICITY, MALLEABLE, PLIABLE:
Flexible; easily shaped, especially by outside influences or forces

The 17th century English philosopher John Locke argued that at birth the human mind is a blank tablet (a *tabula rasa*) and that, as a result, all of our ideas are shaped by experience. Locke thus believed that humans are by nature MALLEABLE. Modern public relations specialists have extended Locke's view to include the belief that public opinion is highly PLASTIC and can thus be shaped. For example, in the movie *Hancock*, Hancock is a SURLY (Word 361) superhero who is so disliked that most people in Los

Angeles want him to leave their city. However, Ray Embrey is a public relations specialist who is determined to transform Hancock's image. Embrey's faith in the PLASTICITY of public opinion proves to be justified. Popular attitudes prove to be PLIABLE, and after he saves a policeman's life, Hancock becomes a popular hero.

318. CHAGRIN:
The feeling of distress caused by humiliation, failure or embarrassment

In the movie *Anchorman*, Brian Fantana is CHAGRINED when he discovers that his cologne is so foul smelling that it repels Veronica and everyone else in the newsroom. In the movie *Pretty Woman*, Vivian is deeply CHAGRINED when SUPERCILIOUS (Word 370) clerks in a fashionable clothing store refuse to help her because of the way she is dressed.

319. OBSTREPEROUS:
Noisily and stubbornly defiant; unruly; boisterous

The television program *Supernanny* features Jo Frost's amazing ability to tame even the wildest and most OBSTREPEROUS children. If you watch *Desperate Housewives*, you know that Lynette and her husband could use help from the Supernanny to discipline their four OBSTREPEROUS children.

320. IDYLLIC:
Charmingly simple and carefree

What do Happy Land in *Happy Gilmore* and Andalasia in *Enchanted* have in common? Both are charming, IDYLLIC places. Happy Land is an imaginary place where Happy can relax with Virginia and forget about Shooter McGavin. Andalasia is an IDYLLIC paradise where magical creatures and humans all live carefree blissful lives.

321. DILAPIDATED:
Having fallen into a state of disrepair; broken-down; in deplorable condition

In his autobiography *Black Boy*, Richard Wright provides a vivid description of the nightmare of living in a DILAPIDATED home furnished with broken furniture and filthy kitchen appliances. President Johnson's Great Society included urban renewal projects designed to rebuild DILAPIDATED neighborhoods like the ones Richard Wright lived in.

322. EXTEMPORIZE and IMPROVISE:
Both mean to lecture or speak without notes

Dr. King's "I Have a Dream" speech is one of the most ACCLAIMED (Word 91) orations in American history. Yet most people are unaware of the fact that Dr. King EXTEMPORIZED most of the speech. After beginning with his prepared text, Dr. King IMPROVISED saying, "We will not be satisfied until justice runs down like waters and righteousness like a mighty stream." Knowing that Dr. King had wandered from his prepared text, the renowned gospel singer Mahalia Jackson urged him to continue shouting out, "Tell 'em about the dream, Martin." Dr. King then began the EXTEMPORIZED "Dream" sequence that GAL-VANIZED (WORD 148) his audience and inspired the nation.

323. MYRIAD:
Many; numerous

In *Harry Potter and the Half-Blood Prince*, MYRIAD problems test Harry during his sixth year at Hogwarts. Harry's challenges include retrieving a key memory from Professor Slughorn, dealing with his romantic feelings for Ginny, helping Professor Dumbledore destroy Lord Voldemort's Horcruxes, and THWARTING (Word 67) Draco Malfoy's sinister scheme. Harry must draw upon all of his skills as a wizard to successfully meet the demands posted by these MYRIAD tasks.

324. UNGAINLY:
Awkward; clumsy

What do Mia Thermopolis (*Princess Diaries*) and Betty Suarez (*Ugly Betty*) have in common? Both are AFFABLE (Word 18) but UNGAINLY young women. Mia is the 15-year-old heir to the throne of the fictional kingdom of Genovia. She attends an exclusive private school and is regularly teased by her peers for her UNGAINLY manners and frizzy hair. Betty works at the ultra-chic New York City fashion magazine *Mode*. She is good-hearted, but her thick-framed glasses and prominent set of extra-large dental braces underscore her UNGAINLY appearance.

325. DILATORY:
Habitually late; tardy

I'm here to inspire,
Now is not the time to tire.
You're doing fine,
It's near the end of Chapter Nine.

DILATORY means late,
So control your own fate.
Don't delay,
Study our words each day!

Grand Master Larry is right. Don't be DILATORY! Remember Emperor Charlemagne in Word 219? His strategy of trying to learn words by OSMOSIS proved to be FUTILE (Word 46). A more effective approach is to study a few words every day. Repetition is important. You might go to the Fast Review at the end of this volume and put a check beside each word you have learned. That will help mark your progress and let you know which words to spend more time on. Above all, don't be DILATORY!

326. VITUPERATIVE:

Characterized by verbal abuse; bitter criticism

Most critics panned Britney Spears' INEPT (Word 114) performance at the VMA Awards Show. While some reviewers attempted to provide the former Pop Princess with constructive criticism, others wrote critiques that were astonishingly VITUPERATIVE. Here are some examples of their VITUPERATIVE critique of Britney's performance:

- "Britney's wig, much like her talent, isn't real."

- "Zoned-out Britney was a flop."

- "How about the simple and final confirmation that she just can't sing."

327. DISCORDANT:

Not in harmony; incompatible; at variance with, as in a DISCORDANT detail that doesn't fit a pattern

In *The Cornish Trilogy*, Francis Cornish is an art expert who specializes in finding DISCORDANT details to prove that a painting is not authentic. Cornish demonstrates his amazing powers of observation and command of ESOTERIC (Word 369) facts when he evaluates a painting thought to be by the 15th century Dutch master Hubert van Eyck. The painting included a monkey hanging by its tail from the bars of Hell. This seemingly INNOCUOUS (Word 99) image proved to be a DISCORDANT detail. Monkeys with prehensile tails did not exist in Europe until the 16th century. Since van Eyck died in 1426, the painting had to be a forgery!

328. PERFIDIOUS:

Treacherous; traitorous; deceitful

What do Judas Iscariot, Ephialtes, Benedict Arnold, and Peter Pettigrew have in common? All four were PERFIDIOUS traitors and opportunists. Judas betrayed Christ, Ephialtes betrayed the Spartans, Benedict Arnold betrayed the Colonial Army, and Peter Pettigrew ("Wormtail") betrayed James and Lily Potter.

329. PROLIFERATION:

To rapidly increase

Pop and rap have traditionally been separate musical categories. But that DICHOTOMY (division into contrasting parts) is disappearing. There is now a PROLIFERATION of songs that blend rapping and singing. For example, Katy Perry;s hit *California Gurls* features Snoop Dogg and Justin Bieber's hit *Baby* features Ludacris.

330. INDOMITABLE and RESOLUTE:
Very determined; unwavering

The Buffalo Bills' tight end Kevin Everett suffered a severe spinal cord injury while making a tackle in the opening game of the 2007 NFL season. Everett was paralyzed from the neck down when he arrived at the hospital. Doctors feared that Everett would never walk again. But Everett remained RESOLUTE. State-of-the-art medical care and his own INDOMITABLE spirit gave Everett the will to fight every day for recovery. Remarkably, Everett is now able to walk again. His courage and RESOLUTE attitude have inspired others who have suffered similar injuries.

331. MORIBUND:
Approaching death; about to become obsolete

As the year CE 476 began, the once invincible Roman Empire was a MORIBUND remnant of its once-great self. Germanic tribes overran its western provinces, while the Ostrogoths invaded Italy. Sacked by the Vandals in CE 455, Rome's broken aqueducts, shattered monuments, and looted temples were mere shadows of their former glory. The last Roman emperor was a 14-year-old boy whose name, Romulus Augustulus, recalled 1000 years of past grandeur. Recognizing that the emperor was powerless and that his empire was MORIBUND, a barbarian general named Odoacer dismissed the boy emperor, thus finalizing "the fall of the Roman Empire."

Tip for a Direct Hit

The Latin noun *mors*, meaning "death," can help you remember a number of SAT words. For example, both MOROSE (Word 27) and MORBID mean very depressed and preoccupied with death. A person who is MORTIFIED is literally "dying from embarrassment." While Lord Voldemort will probably not be on your SAT, his name includes *mor* and means "flight from death."

332. NUANCE:
A SUBTLE (Word 96) shade of meaning or feeling; a slight degree of difference

In the movie *Harry Potter and the Half-Blood Prince*, actor Tom Felton portrays Draco Malfoy. The role requires a NUANCED performance. When Lord Voldemort assigns him the mission of killing Albus Dumbledore, Draco feels conflicted. He is torn between his ambition to please Voldemort and a fear that he cannot commit a heinous crime he will always regret. Felton relished the opportunity to portray Draco's NUANCED emotions. "If you're feeling sorry for him," says Felton, "then I've done my job."

333. FLIPPANT and FACETIOUS:
Treating serious matters with lighthearted humor or lack of respect

In the movie *Juno*, Juno MacGuff is an independent-minded teenager confronted with an unplanned pregnancy. Juno hides behind a façade of FLIPPANT wisecracks. For example, when Vanessa Loring, a potential adoptive mother, earnestly reminds Juno that her parents are probably wondering where she is, Juno FLIPPANTLY asks, "Nah... I mean, I'm already pregnant, so what other kind of shenanigans could I get into?" Juno's FACETIOUS remarks BELIE (Word 30) her true feelings of insecurity as she struggles to find a responsible solution for the unintended consequences of her actions.

334. CREDULOUS:

Easily convinced; tending to believe too readily; GULLIBLE

In his famous *Histories*, the ancient Greek historian Herodotus set out to record "wondrous deeds and wars." Herodotus enlivens his pages with fascinating ANECDOTES (Word 213) and illustrations. However, Herodotus is at times overly CREDULOUS. For example, he readily accepted reports of giant ants in India that hoarded gold. Although normally not known for being CREDULOUS, Alexander the Great conducted a FUTILE (Word 46) search for the "gold-digging" ants and their treasure-filled anthills.

335. FLORID:

Flowery in style; very ORNATE (Word 363)

Romance novels are well known for their FLORID prose. Written by Stephanie Meyer, *Twilight* is a popular vampire-romance novel that features FLORID descriptions. Here is a particularly FLORID portrait of Edward Cullen: "He lay perfectly still in the grass, his shirt open over his sculpted, incandescent chest, his SCINTILLATING (Word 382) arms bare. His glistening, pale lavender lids were shut, though of course he didn't sleep." When Edward opened his eyes, he looked at Bella "with a WISTFUL (pensively sad, especially for something yearned for) expression. The golden eyes held mine, and I lost my train of thought."

336. EXCORIATING and SCATHING:
Expressing strong disapproval; condemning; to loudly DECRY (Word 174)

On July 8, 2010, LeBron James used a nationally televised interview to announce his decision to leave the Cleveland Cavaliers and play basketball for the Miami Heat. While jubilant Miami fans celebrated, Cavalier owner Dan Gilbert issued a SCATHING statement EXCORIATING James for his "cowardly betrayal." The APOPLECTIC (furious) owner guaranteed that the Cavaliers would win an NBA Championship before the self-styled former king wins one.

337. INTERLOPER:
An intruder; a gatecrasher

In the movie *Wedding Crashers*, Owen Wilson and Vince Vaughn star as a pair of Washington divorce mediators who spend their spring weekends crashing weddings. The two charming INTERLOPERS always concoct clever back stories to deceive inquisitive quests. After a successful season, the pair of INTERLOPERS infiltrate a particularly LAVISH (Word 363) wedding where Owen unexpectedly falls for one of the bridesmaids.

338. CEREBRAL:
Intellectual rather than emotional

VISCERAL:
Instinctive rather than rational

Do you typically follow your head or your heart? If you follow your head, you have a CEREBRAL or intellectual response to problems. In contrast, if you follow your heart, then you have a VISCERAL or emotional response to problems. The Star Trek movies vividly depict this age-old duality. Spock is a CEREBRAL science officer whose decisions are governed by logic. In contrast, Dr. McCoy is a physician whose decisions are often affected by his gut reactions to a situation.

 Tip for a Direct Hit

The words CEREBRAL and VISCERAL are both derived from parts of the human body. The cerebrum is the main part of the human brain and is associated with thought. Viscera refers to soft internal organs and thus become associated with internal or "gut" feelings.

339. NONPLUSSED and CONFOUNDED:
Utterly PERPLEXED (Word 19); completely puzzled; totally bewildered

On July 14, 1789, a mob successfully stormed a royal fortress in Paris known as the Bastille. The rioters overpowered the guards and seized 20,000 pounds of gunpowder. While these MOMENTOUS (Word 193) events were taking place, King Louis XVI spent an uneventful day hunting. The exhausted monarch returned to the Versailles Palace and went to sleep. The Duc de La Rochefoucauld-Liancourt awakened the sleepy king and reported what had happened at the Bastille. The shocking report left Louis CONFOUNDED. Confused and at a loss for words, Louis finally stammered, "Is this a rebellion?" The Duc emphatically replied, "No sire, it is a revolution."

340. IGNOMINIOUS:
Humiliating; shameful; disgraceful

Almost 1 billion people watched Spain defeat the Netherlands 1 – 0 to capture the 2010 World Cup. The Spanish victory ignited joyous celebrations across Spain. While the triumphant Spanish team received a heroes welcome, the French team returned home in a cargo plane. Furious French soccer fans demanded answers for their team's humiliating failure to win a single match. France's IGNOMINIOUS early exit left the soccer-crazed nation in shock and anger. The nation's leading sports newspaper called the DEBACLE (Word 146) "a State scandal."

Testing Your Vocabulary

Each SAT contains 19 sentence completion questions that are primarily a test of your vocabulary. Each sentence completion will always have a key word or phrase that will lead you to the correct answer. Use the vocabulary from Chapters 6-9 to circle the answer to each of the following 10 sentence completion questions. You'll find answers and explanations on pages 102-103.

1. The female subject of this painting by Henri Matisse seems _____, as if Matisse sought to portray an unconquerable female spirit.

    (A) ungainly
    (B) indomitable
    (C) quiescent
    (D) vacuous
    (E) perfidious

2. The coach urged his team's zealous fans to refrain from making any _____ remarks, ones that would be considered disrespectful or disparaging of the visiting team.

    (A) perfunctory
    (B) provisional
    (C) contiguous
    (D) anecdotal
    (E) slighting

3. Some people alternate between contrasting temperaments; either they are _____ or they are _____.

   (A) complaisant .. petulant
   (B) indomitable .. resolute
   (C) obdurate .. intractable
   (D) imperious .. domineering
   (E) truculent .. belligerent

4. Daniel Webster's reputation for sublime _____ was reinforced by his learned, authoritative, and even _____ tone when delivering speeches on the Senate floor.

   (A) comedy .. truculent
   (B) diligence .. perfunctory
   (C) oratory .. magisterial
   (D) loyalty .. perfidious
   (E) optimism .. disheartening

5. According to Suetonius, Roman society was _____ and dissolute, for _____ behavior was encouraged by the irresponsible aristocracy.

   (A) gracious .. magisterial
   (B) idyllic .. perfidious
   (C) modest .. imperious
   (D) debauched .. licentious
   (E) duplicitous .. parsimonious

6. The salesman was known for both his _____ and his _____: he lied frequently but did so with great enthusiasm and flair.

   (A) venality .. indifference
   (B) pugnacity .. animation
   (C) petulance .. aloofness
   (D) complicity .. malfeasance
   (E) duplicity .. élan

7. Linduff has an unquestionably _____ manner: she fawns on anyone whom she perceives to be her superior.

    (A) imperious
    (B) inquisitive
    (C) discordant
    (D) belligerent
    (E) subservient

8. Although she was a capable student, Hannah typically engaged in _____ study habits by not preparing for her final exams until the last possible moment.

    (A) dilatory
    (B) superfluous
    (C) unprecedented
    (D) obstreperous
    (E) craven

9. Brianna was a friendly and conciliatory person; she had none of her brother's _____.

    (A) pugnacity
    (B) affability
    (C) venality
    (D) élan
    (E) extravagance

10. The now disgraced governor was _____ public official, who was corrupt and easily bribed.

    (A) a vituperative
    (B) an obdurate
    (C) a venal
    (D) an imperious
    (E) a craven

Answers and Explanations

1. **B**

   The question asks you to find a word that is consistent with the key phrase "unconquerable female spirit." The correct answer is INDOMITABLE (Word 330).

2. **E**

   The question asks you to find a word that is consistent with remarks that are "disrespectful and disparaging." The correct answer is SLIGHTING (Word 312).

3. **A**

   The question asks you to find a pair of answers that are opposites since the people "alternate between contrasting temperaments." The correct answer is COMPLAISANT (Word 306) and PETULANT (Word 305). All of the other answer choices were pairs of synonyms.

4. **C**

   The question asks you to find a first word that is consistent with "delivering speeches" and a second word that is consistent with being "learned and authoritative." The correct answer is ORATORY and MAGISTERIAL (Word 316).

5. **D**

   The question asks you to find a first word that is consistent with "dissolute" and a second word that describes a "dissolute" and "irresponsible" aristocracy. The correct answer is DEBAUCHED and LICENTIOUS (Word 293)

6. **E**

The question asks you to find a first word that means "lied frequently" and a second word that means "great enthusiasm and flair." The correct answer is DUPLICITY (Word 296) and ÉLAN (Word 287).

7. **E**

The question asks you to find a word that is consistent with the key word, "fawns." The correct answer is SUBSERVIENT (Word 307).

8. **A**

The question asks you to find a word that describes a student who waits "until the last possible moment" to study for final exams. The correct answer is DILATORY (Word 325).

9. **A**

The question asks you to find a word that means the opposite of "friendly and complaisant." The correct answer is PUGNACITY (Word 285).

10. **C**

The question asks you to find a word describing a "disgraced governor" who "was corrupt and easily bribed." The correct answer is VENAL (Word 292).

Chapter 10

THE TOUGHEST WORDS II: 341–400

Chapter 10 continues our goal of helping you learn the 120 toughest words on the SAT. As in Chapter 9, each of these words was the answer or answer choice to a Level 5 question. You'll find that we have used an ECLECTIC (variety) mix of popular and historic examples to help ELUCIDATE (clarify, explain) the meaning of each word. Our approach is always DIDACTIC (intended to instruct). Don't be CHURLISH (ill-tempered) or REFRACTORY (obstinate). Our SCINTILLATING (sparkling) examples will inspire you to complete the final 60 words. When you finish, you'll be an articulate student who can write forcefully, speak eloquently, and achieve soaring scores on the SAT!

341. IDIOSYNCRASY:
A trait or mannerism that is peculiar to an individual

The cast of MTV's *Jersey Shore* all have distinctive IDIOSYNCRASIES. For example, Sammi "Sweetheart" loves to wear hair extensions, Vinnie loves to fist pump on the dance floor, Michael "The Situation" loves to show off his chiseled abs, and Pauly D loves to use hair gel. Pauly D spends 30 minutes in the morning and another 30 minutes in the evening sculpting his signature blowout hairstyle. Pauly spends $100.00 a week on hair gel. Believe it or not, you can go to a hair salon and ask for a "Pauly D" haircut.

342. CENSORIOUS and CAPTIOUS:
Highly critical; fault-finding

In the movie *Animal House*, the Deltas are a group of BOORISH (Word 64) fraternity brothers who have done their best to provoke the CENSORIOUS Dean of Students, Vernon Wormer. Realizing that for the Deltas, "party animals" is really a EUPHEMISM (an inoffensive word substituted for an offensive word) for "drunken students" the outraged dean vows to expel the Deltas from Faber College. Led by "Otter" and "Boon," the HEDONISTIC (Word 104) Deltas continue to infuriate their CAPTIOUS Dean and he puts the Deltas on "double secret probation." When the Deltas all fail their midterms, Dean Wormer expels them from school and happily notifies their draft boards of their eligibility. UNDAUNTED (Word 73), the Deltas seek revenge by wreaking havoc on Faber College's annual Homecoming parade.

343. CONSTERNATION:
A state of great dismay and confusion

In the movie *Juno*, Juno MacGuff faces many difficult choices. After deciding against getting an abortion, Juno agrees to have a closed adoption with Vanessa and Mark Loring. The Lorings seem like the perfect couple because they are young and AFFLUENT (Word 231), and Vanessa has her heart set on becoming a mother. With everything seemingly agreed upon, Juno reacts with great CONSTERNATION when Mark later tells her that he has decided to leave Vanessa. Juno ultimately overcomes her CONSTERNATION and stands by her agreement to give her baby to Vanessa.

344. DIDACTIC and EDIFY:
Designed or intended to teach and instruct

In the movie *Dead Poets Society*, John Keating is a gifted but UNORTHODOX (Word 7) teacher at a strict private school. On the first day of class, Keating surprises his students by taking them on a "field trip" to look at former Welton students' photographs hanging in a trophy case. Keating points out that the boys in the old photographs had great dreams: "Their eyes are full of hope, just like you." Keating's purpose is DIDACTIC. He wants to teach his students the idea of *carpe diem* (Latin for "seize the day") by emphasizing that time is fleeting and opportunities must be seized before it is too late. Keating uses this uplifting message to EDIFY his students and prepare them for the themes in his literature course.

345. ELUCIDATE:

To make clear or plain, especially by explanation

In the movie *Dead Poets Society*, John Keating (see Word 344) rejects the textbook's lifeless approach to poetry. Instead he ELUCIDATES an entirely different approach by explaining, "We don't read and write poetry because it's cute. We read and write poetry because we are members of the human race. And the race is filled with passion."

 Tip for a Direct Hit

ELUCIDATE contains the Latin root *luc* meaning light. This useful root shines a beam of light on the difficult Level 5 words LUCID and PELLUCID. LUCID is literally "lit up" and thus "clear" in the sense of being easily understood. It is often paired in sentence completion questions with its antonym CONVOLUTED (Word 75), which means twisted and thus difficult to understand. PELLUCID means crystal clear, like the PELLUCID waters of a pure mountain stream.

346. EFFUSIVE:

Unrestrained praise

Movie critics are normally restrained and hard-to-please. However, critics have been overwhelmingly EFFUSIVE in their praise for Christopher Nolan's work as the director of *The Dark Knight*. Praising the film as "an EPIC (Word 208) masterpiece" and "quite possibly the best superhero movie ever made," critics have LAUDED (Word 91) Nolan for superbly crafted scenes that include innovative sequences shot using Imax cameras and breathtaking VERTIGINOUS (Word 368) mid-air escapes. Reviewers have not limited their EFFUSIVE praise to Nolan's ADROIT (Word 67) cinematic techniques. They have also commended his ability to create complex characters that embody the moral AMBIGUITIES (Word 21) of a city with a constant tension between good and evil.

347. PROLIFIC:
Very productive

What do the British novelist J. K. Rowling and the American rapper Lil Wayne have in common? At first glance, this may seem like an odd JUXTAPOSITION (side by side comparison). However, both Rowling and Lil Wayne are very successful, popular, and PROLIFIC. Rowling's seven volume SAGA (Word 208) contains over 4000 pages. Lil Wayne is a prolific rapper who recorded his first hit when he was just fifteen. *Rolling Stone* magazine calls the rap megastar "a 24-hour-a-day recording machine."

348. FUROR:
A general commotion; an uproar

In March 2009, AIG announced that the insurance company would be paying out $165 million in executive bonuses. Normally this news would have merited little or no public notice. But this was not a routine announcement. AIG had already received

$185 billion from American taxpayers to cover the company's enormous losses. The bonuses ignited widespread public FUROR. Irate taxpayers deluged Congress with emails and phone calls LAMBASTING (Word 336) AIG. Senator Shelby of Alabama expressed the public FUROR when he said, "These people brought this on themselves. Now you're rewarding failure. A lot of these people should be fired, not awarded bonuses. This is horrible. It's outrageous."

349. PARANOIA:
A tendency on the part of an individual or group toward excessive or irrational suspiciousness; irrational fear

Do you have any irrational fears? If so, you are not alone. Many celebrities have confessed to being PARANOID about a variety of everyday things. For example, Cameron Diaz refuses to touch door handles with her bare hands. Although Daniel Radcliffe may play the world's most popular wizard, he has a PARANOID reaction to clowns. Johnny Depp and P. Diddy also share Radcliffe's PARANOIA about circus entertainers.

350. MARGINAL and PERIPHERAL:
Of secondary importance; NOT central

Everyone agrees that Harry, Hermione, and Ron are central characters in the Harry Potter SAGA (Word 208). But can you identify Hannah Abbott? Probably not. Hannah was a MARGINAL character who was a member of Hufflepuff and Dumbledore's Army. As an adult, she became the wife of Neville Longbottom and the landlady of the Leaky Cauldron.

Tip for a Direct Hit

It is important to note that MARGINAL gives us the word MARGINALIZE. As you might guess, MARGINALIZE means to be relegated to a position of secondary importance.

351. OBFUSCATE:

To deliberately confuse; to make something so confusing that it is hard to understand

In the movie *Shrek*, Lord Farquaad captured the Gingerbread Man and demanded to know who was hiding the remaining fairy-tale characters. But the valiant Gingerbread Man cleverly OBFUSCATED the truth:

Lord Farquaad:	Who is hiding them?
Gingerbread Man:	OK, I'll tell you. Do you know the Muffin Man?
Lord Farquaad:	The Muffin Man?
Gingerbread Man:	The Muffin Man!
Lord Farquaad:	Yes, I know the Muffin Man who lives on Drury Lane.
Gingerbread Man:	Well, she's married to the Muffin Man.
Lord Farquaad:	The Muffin Man?
Gingerbread Man:	The Muffin Man!
Lord Farquaad:	She's married to the Muffin Man!

352. FLUMMOX:
To confuse; perplex

What do viewers of the television series *Lost* and the movie series *Matrix* have in common? Both series have CONVOLUTED plots (see Word 75) that left many viewers FLUMMOXED. Viewers of *Lost* and *Matrix* were not the only ones left FLUMMOXED by the twists and turns of a complicated plot. The Gingerbread Man's clever OBFUSCATION (see Word 351) left Lord Farquaad FLUMMOXED.

353. SPATE:
A large number or amount

Each spring, fans of action adventure movies eagerly await the arrival of new blockbuster films. Hollywood did not disappoint fans in the summer of 2010. Studios produced a SPATE of popular action adventure films including *Iron Man 2*, *Robin Hood*, *The A-Team*, and *Prince of Persia: The Sands of Time*.

354. INEFFABLE:
A feeling that cannot be put into words; indescribable

What do Josie (*Never Been Kissed*) and Giselle (*Enchanted*) have in common? Both experienced a special and thus INEFFABLE first kiss. Josie's IN-EFFABLE moment occurred when Mr. Coulson kissed her on the pitcher's mound in front of most of the student body. Giselle's INEFFABLE moment occurred when she shared true love's first kiss with Prince Edward.

355. HISTRIONIC and OVERWROUGHT:
Excessively dramatic; a deliberate display of emotion

Suppose you are walking on the boardwalk with your boyfriend and he pointed to your feet and said, "You have Fred Flintstone big toes!" Would you ignore the comment, respond with MEASURED (restrained) sarcasm, or throw a HISTRIONIC fit? When this happened on MTV's *Jersey Shore*, Sammi "Sweetheart" predictably became OVERWROUGHT and briefly broke up with Ronnie.

356. PLACATE:
To soothe or calm; appease

In the movie *Clueless*, Cher reacts with great CONSTERNATION (Word 343) when she discovers that Mr. Hall has given her a C in debate. Cher skillfully PLACATES her father by claiming that "some teachers are trying to low-ball me." As the daughter of a high-powered lawyer, Cher views her grades as "a first offer" and promises to use them as "a jumping-off point to start negotiations." PLACATED by Cher's strategy, her father agrees to wait. His patience is rewarded when Cher successfully argues her way from a C to an A-.

357. ESCHEW:
To avoid; shun; stay clear of

What do the beatniks of the 1950s and the hippies of the 1960s have in common? Both ESCHEWED the conventional middle-class lifestyle of their times. The beatniks ESCHEWED conformity and materialism.

Preferring to pursue a more communal lifestyle, the hippies ESCHEWED commercialism and competition.

358. STOPGAP:
A temporary solution designed to meet an urgent need

The Great Depression confronted the United States with an UNPRECEDENTED (Word 259) economic crisis. During the famous Hundred Days, Congress responded by passing a series of emergency bills. Critics promptly attacked the National Industrial Recovery Act (NIRA), the Agricultural Adjustment Act (AAA), and other New Deal programs by calling them STOPGAP measures that at best provided only short-term relief. Historians now argue that the New Deal included both long-term reforms such as Social Security and STOPGAP programs that MITIGATED (Word 31) but did not end the Depression.

359. FLOTSAM:
The floating wreckage of a ship; debris

According to legend, the Kraken was a huge, many-armed creature that could reach as high as the top of a sailing ship's main mast. In *Pirates of the Caribbean: Dead Man's Chest*, the Kraken destroyed the *Black Pearl*, leaving only scattered FLOTSAM floating on the ocean surface.

While FLOTSAM typically refers to floating wreckage, it can also refer to cosmic debris. For example, the asteroid Eugenia is one of thousands of bits of cosmic FLOTSAM in the great asteroid belt between the orbits of the planets Mars and Jupiter.

360. RESTITUTION:

The act of making good or compensating for a loss, damage or injury

In 1942, the U.S. Army's Western Defense Command ordered the forced evacuation of 110,000 Japanese-Americans living on the Pacific Coast. Fearing that they might act as SABOTEURS (subversive agents) for Japan, the government ordered Japanese Americans to pack up their belongings and move to "relocation centers" hastily erected farther inland. Forty-six years later, the U.S. government officially apologized for its action and approved a RESTITUTION payment of $20,000 to each camp survivor.

361. CHURLISH, SULLEN, SURLY:

All three mean ill-tempered; rude; lacking civility

What do Landon Carter (*A Walk to Remember*) and Hancock (*Hancock*) have in common? Both are initially CHURLISH characters who ultimately become more mature. In the opening scenes of *A Walk to Remember*, Landon is a CHURLISH teenager who hangs out with an equally SULLEN group of immature friends who lack direction, goals, and any form of faith. In the opening scenes of *Hancock*, Hancock is a SURLY superhero who is DISHEVELED (unkempt, messy), perpetually drunk, and despised by little children.

362. DISQUIETING:

Disturbing; upsetting; causing unease

In the movie *A Walk to Remember*, Landon falls in love with Jamie and is transformed from a CHURL-

ISH BOOR into a sensitive person who is beginning to find himself (see Word 361). But Landon receives a severe jolt when Jamie reveals some very DISQUIETING information about her health. She has leukemia and has stopped responding to treatment. Although shocked by Jamie's DISQUIETING story, Landon's love nonetheless remains steadfast.

363. ORNATE:
Characterized by elaborate and expensive decorations; LAVISH

During the 1930's, 85 million Americans a week watched a movie at their local movie palace. The ORNATE movie palaces boasted LAVISH decorations and elaborate lobbies where people could escape from the hard times of the Great Depression. The "Fabulous Fox" in Atlanta, for example, featured fantasy architecture, the second-largest theatre organ in the world, and luxurious light fixtures and furniture purchased by the owner's wife. Today, enormous multiplexes have SUPPLANTED (replaced) the old ORNATE movie palaces. Interestingly, a grass-roots campaign led by local high school students saved the Fox. Today, the ORNATE building is a National Historic Landmark and a successful multi-purpose performing arts center.

364. EXECRABLE, ODIOUS, REPUGNANT:
Detestable; repulsive; extremely bad

In the movie *The Dark Knight*, the Joker is a maniacal fiend who delights in committing EXECRABLE crimes that terrorize Gotham City. Unlike most criminals, the Joker is not motivated by money or greed. Instead, he is a criminal mastermind who commits ODIOUS crimes for pleasure. A CALLOUS (Word 72) fiend who is DEVOID (Word 180) of any morality, the Joker gleefully takes pleasure in the chaos he creates. To the REPUGNANT clown prince of crime, a knife is preferable to a gun, since it enables the Joker to "savor the moment."

365. PERSPICACIOUS, PRESCIENT, DISCERNING:
All three words mean insightful and perceptive

What do the French political writer Alexis de Tocqueville and the Jedi Master Yoda have in common? Both were unusually PERSPICACIOUS. De Tocqueville visited the United States in 1831 and published his observations four years later. De Tocqueville PRESCIENTLY predicted that the debate over slavery would tear the Union apart and that the United States and Russia were destined to be rivals. Like de Tocqueville, Yoda was also an unusually DISCERNING observer of human nature. For example, Yoda was PERSPICACIOUS when he realized that the young Anakin Skywalker could be seduced by the dark side of the Force. Yoda's PRESCIENT insight proved true when Anakin became the villainous Darth Vader.

366. ECLECTIC:
Choosing or using a variety of sources

A person with ECLECTIC taste in music would like Beethoven, Akon, Linkin Park, Rihanna, Carrie Underwood, and Shakira. Similarly, a teacher with an ECLECTIC repertoire of lesson strategies might play DVDs, assign internet projects, hold debates, and give lectures.

367. HIATUS:
An interruption in time or continuity; a break

During the 1980s, Harrison Ford starred in three hugely successful movies featuring the adventures of Indiana Jones. After a 19-year HIATUS, Indy finally returned as the world's best-known archaeologist in *Indiana Jones and the Kingdom of the Crystal Skull*. Interestingly, executive producer George Lucas and director Steven Spielberg set *Crystal Skull* in 1957, exactly 19 years after the events in *Indiana Jones and the Last Crusade*. Thus, the HIATUS in the movies paralleled the HIATUS in the real-world.

368. VERTIGINOUS:
Characterized by or suffering from dizziness; having VERTIGO

What do the films *Blair Witch Project* and *Cloverfield* have in common? Although fictional, both films are presented as documentaries pieced together from amateurish footage. As a result, both films left many movie goers feeling VERTIGINOUS. This VERTIGINOUS effect was particularly pronounced in *Cloverfield*. Shot and edited to look as if filmed with a hand-held camera, *Cloverfield* included numerous jump-cuts that created a sense of VERTIGO, especially among those who sat near the screen.

369. ESOTERIC and ARCANE:
Characterized by knowledge that is known only to a small group of specialists; obscure

Have you ever heard of the Resolute Desk located in the Oval Office of the White House? Most people know little or nothing about the desk. But Benjamin Franklin Gates is not a typical person. In the movies

National Treasure and *National Treasure: Book of Secrets*, Gates, a renowned treasure hunter, is a storehouse of ESOTERIC information. Ben demonstrated his knowledge of ARCANE facts by explaining that the Resolute Desk was made from wood from the British warship HMS Resolute and then given to President Hayes by Queen Victoria. Gates further demonstrated his knowledge of ESOTERIC details when he explained that FDR placed a panel in front of the desk to prevent visitors from seeing his leg braces.

370. SUPERCILIOUS:
Haughty disdain, arrogant superiority

On *Gossip Girl*, Leighton Meester plays the spoiled, devious, and SUPERCILIOUS princess Blair Waldorf. Ironically, as a teenager Leighton had to endure the haughty stares of SUPERCILIOUS classmates at Beverly Hills High School. The SUPERCILIOUS real-life 90210 students made fun of Leighton because she didn't wear designer clothes or drive an expensive car. "I wasn't very trendy," Leighton now admits. "I didn't wear makeup and dressed in jeans and T-shirts."

 Tip for a Direct Hit

The Latin prefix *super* means "above." So Superman has powers above those of mortal men. SUPERCILIOUS people are arrogant and haughty because they think they are above others. The prefix *super* can also be seen in the word SUPERFLUOUS (Word 295), which means above what is necessary and therefore extra.

371. CUPIDITY:
Excessive greed, especially for wealth; covetous

The movie *The Third Man*, takes place in Austria's capital city, Vienna. The city and its citizens are struggling to recover from the devastating effects of World War II. Consumed by CUPIDITY, Harry Lime steals penicillin from military hospitals and then sells diluted doses for EXORBITANT (Word 162) prices. The ADULTERATED (debased) antibiotic kills or cripples many of the children who use it. The film's hero, a pulp fiction writer named Joseph Cotten, confronts Lime as they ride on Vienna's famous Ferris wheel. From the top of the Ferris wheel, the people below look like tiny dots. Lime looks down and CALLOUSLY (Word 72) says, "Tell me, would you really feel any pity if one of these dots stopped moving forever? If I offered you $20,000 for every dot that you stopped, would you really tell me to keep my money, or would you calculate how many dots you could afford to spare?" Appalled by Lime's CUPIDITY, Cotten agrees to help police capture his villainous former friend.

372. UNDERWRITE:
To assume financial responsibility for

The Bill and Melinda Gates Foundation is the largest charitable foundation in the world. Its endowment of $38.7 billion dollars enables the foundation to UNDERWRITE numerous projects in the United States and around the world. For example, the Gates Millennium Scholars fund UNDERWRITES a one billion dollar program to provide scholarships for outstanding minority students.

373. DISCOMFITED:
Uneasy;in a state of embarrassment

In the movie *Princess Diaries*, Mia is a shy tenth grade student who attends a private school in San Francisco. Mia is shocked when she discovers that she is heir to the throne of Genovia, a small European principality ruled by her grandmother, Queen Clarisse. Persuaded to attend "princess lessons," Mia feels DISCOMFITED as she learns the etiquette of being a princess. Mia's feelings of DISCOMFITURE become even greater when she attends her school's annual beach party and is embarrassed both when Josh deliberately kisses her in front of a group of photographers and when Lana helps photographers take pictures of her clad only in a towel.

374. TACITURN:
Habitually quiet; uncommunicative

Have you watched the movies *Clerks*, *Clerks II*, *Chasing Amy*, *Mall Rats*, or *Jay and Silent Bob Strike Back*? All of these movies feature a character named Silent Bob. Silent Bob smokes too much, often wears a long coat and a backward baseball cap, and as his nickname suggests, seldom talks and is thus TACITURN. Silent Bob usually relies on hand gestures and facial expressions to communicate his feelings. Although normally TACITURN, Silent Bob offers ASTUTE (perceptive, shrewd) observations on the few occasions when he does speak.

375. SINECURE:
An office or position that requires little or no work and that usually provides an income

In the movie *Batman Begins,* Bruce Wayne is a billionaire businessman who lives in Gotham City. To the world at large, Wayne holds a SINECURE at Wayne Enterprises that enables him to act as an irresponsible, SUPERFICIAL playboy (see Word 90) who lives off his family's personal fortune. Of course, this SINECURE and the Bruce Wayne persona are masks that enable Wayne to hide his secret identity as the Caped Crusader, Batman.

376. LUGUBRIOUS:
Sad and mournful music

In *Star Wars: Episode III Revenge of the Sith,* Padme's death and funeral are accompanied by a LUGUBRIOUS musical score. Similarly, in *Titanic* the musicians play a LUGUBRIOUS hymn as the great but doomed ship slowly sinks into the Atlantic Ocean.

377. COSMOPOLITAN:
Worldly; sophisticated; open-minded and aware of the big picture

PROVINCIAL, PAROCHIAL, INSULAR:
Limited in perspective; narrow; restricted in scope and outlook

Pretend that you are the editor of a newspaper serving a community of 75,000 people. A local middle school teacher has just been named the city's "teacher of the year." At the same time, a story has just come into your office describing changing admission standards in the nation's top universities and colleges. Which story would you place on your paper's front page? Your decision will probably depend upon whether you have a COSMOPOLITAN or a PROVINCIAL outlook. A COSMOPOLITAN editor would favor a "big picture" outlook and give precedence to the national story. A PROVINCIAL editor would favor a local story.

Tip for a Direct Hit

The contrast between COSMOPOLITAN and PROVINCIAL outlooks can be traced back to their origins. COSMOPOLITAN is derived from the Greek words *kosmos* or "world" and *polites* or "citizen." So a COSMOPOLITAN person is literally a citizen of the world. In contrast, a province is an outlying part of an empire or nation, so a PROVINCIAL person would have a more limited perspective. Note that PAROCHIAL and INSULAR are synonyms that refer to a narrow outlook. PAROCHIAL is derived from parish, a small administrative unit with just one pastor, and INSULAR is derived from the Latin word *insula* meaning island.

378. FECUND:
Intellectually productive or inventive

What do George Lucas and J.K. Rowling have in common? Both have unusually FECUND imaginations. In his Star Wars SAGA (Word 208), George Lucas created an intergalactic empire populated by humans, alien creatures, robotic droids, Jedi Knights, and Sith Lords. In her Harry Potter SAGA, J.K. Rowling created a secret magical world populated by wizards, witches, dragons, goblins, giants, and elves.

379. OSTENTATIOUS:

Showy; intended to attract notice; pretentious

Wearing OSTENTATIOUS jewelry has a long history. Egyptian pharaohs, European rulers, and Mughal sultans all enjoyed wearing OSTENTATIOUS jewelry. For example, Queen Elizabeth I's wardrobe included 2,000 RESPLENDENT (dazzling) jewel-covered gowns and a diamond-covered tiara.

The passion for wearing OSTENTATIOUS jewelry has not gone out of fashion. Commonly referred to as "bling-bling," OSTENTATIOUS jewelry is a hallmark of hip-hop culture. For example, Rick Ross is well known for his OSTENTATIOUS jewelry. The "Big Boss" recently purchased a chain featuring a pendant with an image of himself. The eye-catching piece includes Ross's trademark shades and reportedly cost $200,000.

380. GUILE:

Treacherous cunning; skillful deceit

What do Supreme Chancellor Palpatine (*Star Wars Episode III: Revenge of the Sith*), King Edward I (*Braveheart*), and Cher (*Clueless*) all have in common? They all use GUILE to achieve their goals. Supreme Chancellor Palpatine uses GUILE to deceive Anakin, King Edward I uses GUILE to capture William Wallace, and Cher uses GUILE to trick Mr. Hall into falling in love with Ms. Guise so that he will be blissfully happy and thus raise everyone's grades.

381. SANGUINE:
Cheerfully confident; optimistic

In the movie *Enchanted*, Giselle is a beautiful maiden who lives in the IDYLLIC (Word 320) land of Andalasia. Giselle meets and falls in love with handsome Prince Edward. However, their marriage plans are THWARTED (Word 68) when villainous Queen Narissa banishes Giselle to a place where there are no happily ever afters – Times Square in modern New York City. Despite this setback, Giselle remains surprisingly SANGUINE. She is confident that Prince Edward will rescue her and take her back to Andalasia.

382. SCINTILLATING:
Sparkling; shining; brilliantly clever

In the TV show *Glee*, Spanish teacher Will Schuester hopes to REVITALIZE (restore vitality) his high school's MORIBUND (Word 331) glee club. In the beginning, the struggling club consists of an ECLECTIC (Word 366) group of school outcasts that includes fame-hungry Rachel Berry, FLAMBOYANT (Word 81) Kurt Hummel, DIFFIDENT (Word 11) Tina Cohen-Chang, and paraplegic Artie Abrams.

UNDAUNTED (Word 73) by these challenges, Mr. Schue proves to be a resourceful MENTOR (Word 110) who successfully CAJOLES (coaxes) other talented students to join the new club. Now renamed New Directions, the REJUVENATED (Word 171) club soon performs SCINTILLATING renditions of Journey's "Don't Stop Believing" and Lady Gaga's "Bad Romance."

383. PRISTINE:
Remaining in a pure state; uncorrupted by civilization

Sandwiched between Latin American giants Venezuela and Brazil, Guyana is a small country with a vital global asset. About 80 percent of the country is covered by a PRISTINE rainforest called the Guyana Shield. The Shield is one of only four intact PRISTINE rain forests left on the planet. It is home to 1,400 vertebrate species, 1,680 bird species, and some of the world's most-endangered species, including the jaguar, anaconda, and giant anteater. In a ground-breaking agreement, the government of Guyana announced that it will place over one million acres of PRISTINE rainforest under the protection of a British-led international body in return for development aid.

384. RAMPANT:
Unrestrained; unchecked

While Guyana is taking steps to protect its rainforest, the once PRISTINE (Word 383) Amazon rainforest is being dramatically reduced by RAMPANT develop-ment led by cattle ranchers and loggers. Unless this RAMPANT deforestation is ARRESTED (Word 261), the Amazon rainforest will be reduced by 40 percent in the next 20 years, resulting in the irreversible loss of thousands of species of plants and animals.

385. PERNICIOUS:
Highly injurious; destructive; deadly

Francisco Santos, the Vice-President of Columbia, launched an international campaign to warn people about the PERNICIOUS consequences of cocaine trafficking. Santos made an example of Kate Moss, the British supermodel photographed allegedly snorting cocaine. "When she snorted a line of cocaine, she put land mines in Columbia, she killed people in Columbia, she displaced people in Columbia," Santos told a concerned audience. The PERNICIOUS consequences of cocaine trafficking also extend to the environment. "She destroyed the environment," Santos continued. "We have lost two million hectares (about five million acres) of PRISTINE (Word 383) rain forest to drug trafficking."

386. OBLIVIOUS:

Lacking conscious awareness; unmindful; unaware

A Staten Island teenager named Alexa Longueira learned the meaning of OBLIVIOUS and MALODOROUS (Word 199) the hard way. While walking down a neighborhood street, Alexa was so busy texting that she failed to notice an open manhole in front of her. The OBLIVIOUS high schooler suddenly fell five feet into a pool of MALODOROUS sewage. Fortunately, Alexa only suffered a few minor cuts and bruises. Her accident is a MALODOROUS reminder that you should not be OBLIVIOUS to your surroundings as you focus on texting messages.

387. REFRACTORY:

Obstinately resistant to authority or control

Do you believe that it is possible to create a utopian community? From the Puritan communities at Massachusetts Bay to the hippie communes in the 1960s, many people have tried and failed to create utopias. While there are many reasons why utopian communities have failed, the sheer REFRACTORI-NESS of human nature is a leading cause. Petty quarrels and jealous disputes provide all-too-common examples of REFRACTORY behavior that undermines even the most ideal group goals.

388. GARRULOUS, VERBOSE, LOQUACIOUS:
Annoyingly talkative; VOLUBLE

What do Donkey in all three *Shrek* movies and Seth in *Superbad* have in common? Both are very GAR-RULOUS. Donkey often exasperates Shrek with his VERBOSE chatter. And Seth is so LOQUACIOUS that it is difficult to think of a time when he isn't talking.

389. CONVIVIAL:
Fond of feasting, drinking, and good company

What do the Deltas in *Animal House* and Ben and his friends in *Knocked Up* have in common? They are all CONVIVIAL slackers who love to eat, drink, and party. In fact, Ben and his CONVIVIAL buddies are really only NUANCED (Word 332) older versions of Bluto and his CONVIVIAL fraternity brothers.

390. BRUSQUE and CURT:
Abrupt in manner or speech; discourteously blunt

What do Donald Trump, Dr. House, and Montgomery bus driver J.F. Blake have in common? All three share the trait of being BRUSQUE. In the reality show *The Apprentice*, Donald Trump is BRUSQUE when he tells each week's losing apprentice, "You're fired!" Dr. House (*House M.D.*) is a medical genius who is very impatient and CURT with young doctors who misdiagnose an illness. And finally, J.F. Blake PRECIPITATED (Word 253) the Montgomery Bus Boycott when he CURTLY ordered Rosa Parks to give up her seat.

391. TEPID:
Lukewarm; mild; half-hearted

The word TEPID originated in the Roman baths. Bathers soaked in the hot waters of the *caldarium*, took a cool dip in the *frigidarium*, and finished their day with a refreshing bath in the lukewarm waters of the *tepidarium*. TEPID still retains its meaning of being lukewarm or mild. It is most often used when describing lukewarm enthusiasm or praise. For example, although movie-goers eagerly anticipated the release of *Terminator Salvation*, the film received TEPID reviews and generated little fan enthusiasm.

392. PROTEAN:
Readily taking on varied forms and meanings

In Greek mythology Proteus was a sea-god who had two unique abilities. First, he was an ORACLE (Word 124) who could foretell the future. Second, he could change his shape to avoid being captured and forced to make predictions. Proteus still lives in the SAT word PROTEAN. Test writers often use PROTEAN in difficult sentence completion questions about viruses that are hard to target because of their ability to mutate. For example, the HIV virus has proven to be particularly difficult to treat because of its PROTEAN nature.

393. SOLICITOUS:
Showing great care and concern; attentive

In *Harry Potter and the Sorcerer's Stone,* Vernon and Petunia Dursley grudgingly raise Harry, depriving him of love and attention. In contrast, they are very SOLICITOUS of their only child, Dudley. While they force Harry to sleep in a tiny closet beneath the staircase, Vernon and Petunia give the spoiled Dudley everything he wants. For example, when an irate Dudley complains that he only received 37 birthday presents, one fewer than the year before, his SOLICITOUS parents promise to buy him two more gifts.

394. DISINGENUOUS:
Not straightforward or CANDID; insincere

What do the leaders of North Korea and Iran have in common? Both have been DISINGENUOUS about the true purpose of their nuclear programs. For years, the North Koreans DISINGENUOUSLY insisted their nuclear program was designed for peaceful purposes. However, in 2009, North Korea tested an atomic weapon and announced that they were now "a full-fledged nuclear power." Iranian leaders have also insisted there nuclear program is totally peaceful. However, critics contend that the Iranians are being DISINGENUOUS and that their true goal is to develop weapons of mass destruction.

395. VENERATE and REVERE:
To regard with great respect; to hold in high esteem

What do George Washington and Nelson Mandela have in common? Both men are VENERATED as statesmen who played indispensable roles in the history of their countries. George Washington is REVERED as a leader who was "First in war, first in peace, and first in the hearts of his countrymen." Nelson Mandela is VENERATED for his long struggle against apartheid and his leadership in helping South Africa become a multi-racial democracy.

396. CONTENTIOUS:

Quarrelsome; argumentative; likely to provoke a controversy; DISPUTATIOUS

Many film critics rank Mel Gibson's *The Passion of the Christ* as the most controversial movie ever made. The film provoked CONTENTIOUS arguments between supporters who praised its unflinching depiction of Christ's suffering and critics who denounced Gibson's biblical interpretations. These CONTENTIOUS arguments provoked a firestorm of publicity that helped the film gross $370 million.

397. PRECLUDE:

To make impossible; to rule out; prevent

In *Harry Potter and the Sorcerer's Stone*, Harry learns that he is a wizard with a tragic past and a prophesied future. Harry's status as "the Chosen One" who must ultimately confront Lord Voldemort PRECLUDES him from having a normal life. As a living legend in the wizard world, Harry is recognized wherever he goes. Unlike Superman and Batman, Harry cannot avoid unwanted attention by adopting a secret persona. He is PRECLUDED from anonymity and must publicly fulfill his destiny.

398. COMPUNCTION, CONTRITION, REMORSE:
All describe feelings of sincere and deep regret

On June 22, 2009, Chris Brown pleaded guilty to assaulting his former girlfriend Rihanna in a February incident. Four weeks later, the R&B singer issued a video apology, saying, "What I did was inexcusable. I am very sad and very ashamed of what I've done." But was this public statement of CONTRITION too little and too late? Opinion polls show that the public is evenly divided between those who believe Brown is truly REMORSEFUL and those who believe his statement of COMPUNCTION is an insincere attempt to revive his faltering career.

399. DEMOGRAPHY:
The study of the characteristics of human populations

What do the TV shows *American Idol*, *Hannah Montana*, and *iCarly* have in common? They are all among the most popular TV series for tweenagers 9 – 14. Tweenagers are a DEMOGRAPHIC group highly prized by clothing, soft drink, and cosmetic companies. Sponsors carefully study the DEMOGRAPHIC characteristics of television viewers as they make multi-million dollar advertising decisions.

Tip for a Direct Hit

DEMOGRAPHY and DEMOGRAPHIC have become popular words on both the SAT and AP tests. For example, AP US History exams often have questions about such DEMOGRAPHIC characteristics as the size and movement of American population groups.

400. APHORISM and AXIOM:

A statement universally accepted as true; a MAXIM

Benjamin Franklin's famous *Autobiography* contains a storehouse of wise APHORISMS. For example, Franklin earnestly warned students that "by failing to prepare, you are preparing to fail." Franklin's AXIOM is still valid. As your SAT vocabulary coach, let me once again implore you to study the words in your *Direct Hits* vocabulary books. Always remember this three-word AXIOM: "Vocabulary! Vocabulary! Vocabulary!" I hope you have enjoyed reading and studying *Direct Hits*. Good luck on your test!

Testing Your Vocabulary

Each SAT contains 19 sentence completion questions that are primarily a test of your vocabulary. Each sentence completion will always have a key word or phrase that will lead you to the correct answer. Use the vocabulary from Chapters 6-10 to circle the answer to each of the following 10 sentence completion questions. You'll find answers and explanations on pages 136-137.

1. Good parenting groups denounced the YouTube video, finding it to be in _____ taste because it included repulsive images and profane language.

    (A) scintillating
    (B) discriminating
    (C) ornate
    (D) execrable
    (E) ineffable

2. The late Isaac Asimov is among the most _____ writers of all time, having written or edited over 500 books.

    (A) paranoid
    (B) sanguine
    (C) dilatory
    (D) prolific
    (E) censorious

3. Matthew was both _____ and _____: he was surly to the point of being rude and arrogant to the point of being obnoxious.

    (A) churlish .. supercilious
    (B) convivial .. imperious
    (C) curt .. histrionic
    (D) verbose .. didactic
    (E) refractory .. sanguine

4. Judy Chicago, an influential contemporary artist, is known for her _____ style, which features an eccentric and highly individualistic interweaving of themes, imagery, and materials.

    (A) pristine
    (B) lugubrious
    (C) idiosyncratic
    (D) apocryphal
    (E) vacuous

5. Parties and other social gatherings benefit from having _____ hosts who provide entertaining company, delicious food, and lively conversation.

    (A) truculent
    (B) refractory
    (C) oblivious
    (D) brusque
    (E) convivial

6. Like all _____ literature, *Aesop's Fables* was intended to teach important moral lessons and inculcate key cultural values.

    (A) didactic
    (B) histrionic
    (C) pristine
    (D) superfluous
    (E) empirical

7. In temperament the two leaders were very different: Janice was convivial, talkative, and at times even _____; in contrast, Sherece was unassuming, guarded, and at times even _____.

    (A) surly .. sullen
    (B) garrulous .. taciturn
    (C) verbose .. effusive
    (D) imperious .. egalitarian
    (E) obstreperous .. censorious

8. Although Caravaggio was a key figure in Rome's emerging new Baroque style of art, he nevertheless perceived himself as being _____ figure with little influence.

    (A) a vital
    (B) a marginal
    (C) an ungainly
    (D) an epic
    (E) a watershed

9. Since many successful composers draw their inspiration from a variety of cultures, styles, and disciplines, their approach could best be called _____.

    (A) refractory
    (B) vertiginous
    (C) histrionic
    (D) idyllic
    (E) eclectic

10. Minimalist sculptors renounced _____ decorations in favor of an extremely spare style that emphasized basic geometric figures.

    (A) stopgap
    (B) execrable
    (C) redolent
    (D) ornate
    (E) insular

Answers and Explanations

1. **D**

    The question asks you to find a word describing a video that contains "repulsive images and profane language." The correct answer is EXECRABLE (Word 364).

2. **D**

    The question asks you to find a word that describes an author who has written or edited over 500 books. The correct answer is PROLIFIC (Word 347).

3. **A**

    The question asks you to find a first word that means "surly" and a second word that means "arrogant." The correct answer is CHURLISH (Word 361) and SUPERCILIOUS (Word 370).

4. **C**

    The question asks you to find a word that describes an artist who is "eccentric" and "highly individualistic." The correct answer is IDIOSYNCRATIC (Word 341).

5. **E**

    The question asks you to find a word describing a host who provides "entertaining company, delicious food and a lively atmosphere." The correct answer is CONVIVIAL (Word 389).

6. A

The question asks you to find a word that means "to teach important moral lessons and inculcate key cultural values." The correct answer is DIDACTIC (Word 344).

7. B

The question asks you to find a first word that means "talkative" and a second word describing a "very different" person who is "guarded." The correct answer is GARRULOUS (Word 388) and TACITURN (Word 374).

8. B

The question asks you to find a word that is the opposite of "key figure" and is consistent with having "little influence." The correct answer is MARGINAL (Word 350).

9. E

The question asks you to find a word that means "variety." The correct answer is ECLECTIC (Word 366).

10. D

The question asks you to find a word that is the opposite of having "a spare style" and "basic geometric forms." The correct answer is ORNATE (Word 363).

Final Review

Testing Your Vocabulary: Final Review

The following 10 sentence completion and five critical reading questions are designed to give you practice using your knowledge of the core vocabulary in Volume 1 and the toughest words in Volume 2. As always, each sentence completion will have a key word or phrase that will lead you to the correct answer. Make sure to circle your answer. You'll find answers and explanations on pages 145-148.

Sentence Completion

1. Art teachers enthusiastically _____ the new clay, saying that its extraordinary _____ enabled students to mold it into almost any shape.

   (A) touted .. buoyancy
   (B) extolled .. plasticity
   (C) expurgated .. eccentricity
   (D) disparaged .. malleability
   (E) reaffirmed .. longevity

2. Olivia was both _____ and _____: she gave generously to charities but was very thrifty when it came to her personal spending.

   (A) cosmopolitan .. parochial
   (B) philanthropic .. venal
   (C) munificent .. parsimonious
   (D) eclectic .. hackneyed
   (E) affable .. craven

3. Theatre producers rejected the impenetrably dense screenplay, saying that its _____ rendered it unsuitable for even its most sophisticated and _____ patrons.

   (A) poignancy .. pompous
   (B) superficiality .. clairvoyance
   (C) subtlety .. pragmatic
   (D) opacity .. cosmopolitan
   (E) serendipity .. discerning

4. The controversial YouTube video elicited _____ responses: some posts were derisive, while other were _____.

    (A) antithetical .. laudatory
    (B) complementary .. dismissive
    (C) fleeting .. maudlin
    (D) nostalgic .. anguished
    (E) unprecedented .. curt

5. The governor's emergency measures were intended as _____, a temporary expedient that called for voluntary water conservation until permanent laws could be put into place.

    (A) a metaphor
    (B) an anecdote
    (C) a conundrum
    (D) an inquisition
    (E) a stopgap

6. Abigail was an affable and _____ woman; she had none of her sister's _____.

    (A) indomitable .. tenacity
    (B) churlish .. amiability
    (C) sullen .. belligerence
    (D) obstinate .. recalcitrance
    (E) genial .. truculence

7. Those unfriendly critics who preferred opera that was _____ and melodious found the music of Christopher Markham jarring and warned that his influence on opera would be _____.

   (A) obstreperous .. lugubrious
   (B) provocative .. platitudinous
   (C) scintillating .. superfluous
   (D) euphonious .. pernicious
   (E) cacophonous .. perfidious

8. Emily's _____ was the inverse of her brother's caution: she was bold to a fault, while he was overly _____.

   (A) audacity .. circumspect
   (B) munificence .. parsimonious
   (C) belligerence .. truculent
   (D) complaisance .. petulant
   (E) verbosity .. loquacious

9. Many scientists view the precipitous decline in the populations of both polar bears and penguins as a _____: an early warning of the deleterious consequences of global warming.

   (A) pretext
   (B) caricature
   (C) portent
   (D) paradigm
   (E) synopsis

10. The late Isaac Asimov was both _____ and
    _____: he wrote voluminously while
    maintaining exacting standards of research.

    (A) didactic .. idiosyncratic
    (B) prolific .. meticulous
    (C) histrionic .. censorious
    (D) discerning .. disquieting
    (E) eclectic .. superficial

Critical Reading

I realized from the beginning that Mr. Williams was a
born teacher. He combined a profound knowledge of
literature with an intuitive understanding of teenage
students. And most of all, he excelled in telling
entertaining anecdotes that illustrated his key points.

11. As described by the author, Mr. Williams comes
    across as

    (A) a confused dilettante
    (B) a talented raconteur
    (C) a revered iconoclast
    (D) an impassioned demagogue
    (E) a clever charlatan

A stunning lack of attention to plot and dialogue are
by far the most egregious flaws that plague a movie
that should never have been filmed, let alone released.

12. The tone of this sentence is best described as

    (A) scathing
    (B) tempered
    (C) archaic
    (D) convivial
    (E) ambiguous

Art historian Marilyn Stokestad argues that in all of known history only three major artists appeared on the scene by themselves: 14th century Renaissance artist Giotto, 17th century Baroque artist Caravaggio, and 20th century Cubist artist Picasso. Every other artist was part of a movement or specific style.

13. The passage indicates that Giotto, Caravaggio, and Picasso are best viewed as

    (A) controversial pundits
    (B) polarizing contemporaries
    (C) inept novices
    (D) historical anomalies
    (E) superficial sycophants

As a dedicated reformer, I.N. Stokes contended against dumbbell tenements, calling them "dirty, overcrowded, degraded places run by exploitive landlords." Stokes' housing reform efforts culminated when, serving on the New York State Tenement House Commission, he co-authored the Tenement House Law of 1901, which required tenements to have a host of new features, including deep backyards, larger rooms, and broad side-courts.

14. I.N. Stokes's attitude toward dumbbell apartments is best described as

    (A) enlightened advocacy
    (B) resolute opposition
    (C) paralyzing ambivalence
    (D) tempered acquiescence
    (E) nostalgic reminiscence

At that time, I was a traveling reporter assigned to Frederickson's Senate campaign. As the days turned into weeks, I heard his basic stump speech dozens of times. I soon became bored as Frederickson endlessly repeated clichés and slogans about standing up to the Russians, cutting government waste, and building a new and better America.

15. The author believed that Frederickson's speeches were

    (A) scintillating
    (B) divisive
    (C) truculent
    (D) supercilious
    (E) trite

Answers and Explanations

1. **B**

    The question asks you to find a positive first word and a second word that is consistent with the phrase "mold it into almost any shape." The correct answer is EXTOLLED (Word 91) and PLASTICITY (Word 317). Note that in Choice D, while MALLEABILITY (Word 317) works for the second blank, DISPARAGED (Word 93) is a negative word that is not consistent with the key word "enthusiastically."

2. **C**

    The question asks you to find a first word that is consistent with giving "generously" to charities and a second word that is consistent with being "thrifty" in her personal spending. The correct answer is MUNIFICENT (Word 232) and PARSIMONIOUS (Word 233).

3. **D**

    The question asks you to find a first word that means "impenetrably dense" and a second word that is consistent with "sophisticated." The correct answer is OPACITY (Word 290) and COSMOPOLITAN (Word 377).

4. **A**

    The question asks you to find a first word that means "opposite" since the second word must be an antonym of the negative word "derisive." The correct answer is ANTITHETICAL (Word 33) and LAUDATORY (Word 91).

5. E

The question asks you to find a word that is consistent with the key phrase "temporary expedient." The correct answer is STOPGAP (Word 358).

6. E

The question asks you to find a positive first word that is a synonym of "affable" and a second word that is an antonym of the first word. The correct answer is GENIAL (Word 18) and TRUCULENCE (Word 285).

7. D

The question asks you to find a first word that is a synonym of "melodious" and a negative second word describing how "unfriendly critics" would view the influence of Markham's "jarring" music. The correct answer is EUPHONIOUS (Word 209) and PERNICIOUS (Word 385).

8. A

The question asks you to find a first word that means "bold" and a second word that is the "inverse" or opposite of "bold." The correct answer is AUDACITY (Word 9) and CIRCUMSPECT (Word 187).

9. C

The question asks you to find a word that is consistent with the key phrase "an early warning." The correct answer is PORTENT (Word 301).

10. **B**

The question asks you to find a first word that is consistent with writing "voluminously" and a second word that means to maintain "exacting standards of research." The correct answer is PROLIFIC (Word 347) and METICULOUS (Word 8).

11. **B**

The passage describes Mr. Williams as a "born teacher" who excels "in telling entertaining anecdotes." The correct answer is therefore B, since "a talented RACONTEUR" (Word 106) is a person who excels in telling anecdotes.

12. **A**

The passage pinpoints "egregious flaws" in a movie that "should never have been filmed." Since the author's tone is harshly critical, the correct answer is A, "SCATHING" (Word 336).

13. **D**

The passage tells you that Giotto, Caravaggio, and Picasso all "appeared on the scene by themselves" and were not "part of a movement or specific style." Since the three artists were atypical, the correct answer is D, "historical ANOMALIES" (Word 2).

14. **B**

The passage tells you that I.N. Stokes was a "dedicated reformer" who "contended against dumbbell tenements." Since "dedicated" supports "resolute" and "contended against" supports "opposition," the correct answer is B, "RESOLUTE (Word 330) opposition."

15. **E**

The passage tells you that Frederickson's "endlessly repeated clichés and slogans" bored the author. Since "clichés and slogans" are unoriginal and overused words, the correct answer is E, "TRITE" (Word 36).

Fast Review

Quick Definitions

Volume 2 contains 200 words, each of which is illustrated with vivid pop culture and historic examples. The Fast Review is designed to provide you with an easy and efficient way to review the definition of each of these words. I recommend that you put a check beside each word that you know. That way you can quickly identify the words that you are having trouble remembering. Focus on each hard-to-remember word by going over its definition, taking another look at the examples in your book, and trying to come up with your own memory tip. For example, take a close look at Word 326, VITUPERATIVE. Mentally take out the letters TUP, and now you have VIPER. A viper is a large venomous snake. The word VITUPERATIVE includes this sense of being vicious and venomous. A VITUPERATIVE critic is filled with bitter criticisms.

Good luck with your review. Remember, don't expect to learn all of these words at once. Frequent repetition is the best way to learn and remember new words.

CHAPTER 6: KEY LITERARY TERMS

201. SYNOPSIS – a brief summary

202. SIMILE – a figure of speech using like or as to compare two unlike things

203. METAPHOR – a figure of speech comparing two unlike things

204. IRONY – things are not what they are said to be or what they seem

205. SATIRE, LAMPOON, PARODY – a work that ridicules human vices and foibles

206. HYPERBOLE – an exaggeration is used for emphasis or effect

207. CARICATURE – a deliberately exaggerated portrait

208. EPIC – a long narrative poem
     SAGA – a long narrative story

209. EUPHONY – soothing, pleasant sound
     CACOPHONY – jarring, grating sound

210. FORESHADOW – suggest or indicate a future action; presage

211. SUBPLOT – a secondary plot in fiction or drama

212. MEMOIR – a personal journal

213. ANECDOTE – a short account of an interesting incident

214. EULOGY – a laudatory speech or written tribute

215. ALLUSION – an indirect or brief reference to a person, place or event

CHAPTER 7: SCIENCE AND THE SOCIAL SCIENCES

216. CATALYST – an agent that provokes or triggers a change
217. CAUSTIC – a stinging or bitter remark
218. CRYSTALLIZE – to give a definite form
219. OSMOSIS – a gradual often unconscious process of assimilation
220. SEDENTARY – settled; not mobile
221. VIRULENT – very toxic or poisonous
222. EMPIRICAL – guided by practical experience and not theory
223. ENTOMOLOGY – the scientific study of insects
224. GESTATE – to conceive and develop in the mind
225. PARADIGM – a framework or model of thought
226. ENTREPRENEUR – a person who organizes and runs a business
227. LUCRATIVE – very profitable
228. EXTRAVAGANT - excessive
229. AVARICE – excessive greed
230. GLUT, PLETHORA, SURFEIT – a surplus
     PAUCITY – a shortage
231. DESTITUTE, IMPOVERISHED, INDIGENT – very poor
     AFFLUENT and OPULENT – very wealthy
232. MUNIFICENT – very generous
233. PARSIMONIOUS – excessively cheap; stingy
234. DEPRECIATION – a decrease in value

235. REMUNERATE – to compensate; a salary

236. ACCORD – a formal agreement

237. ENLIGHTEN – to illuminate

238. APPEASEMENT – to grant concessions to maintain peace

239. NULLIFY – to make null; declare invalid

240. TRIUMVIRATE – a group of three leaders

241. PRETEXT – an excuse; an alleged cause

242. WATERSHED – a critical turning point

243. CONSENSUS – a general agreement

244. AUTOCRAT and DESPOT – a ruler with unlimited power

245. MANIFESTO – a public declaration of beliefs

246. ENFRANCHISE – to receive the right to vote
     DISENFRANCHISE – to lose the right to vote

247. COERCE – to compel someone to do something

248. EGALITARIAN – belief in a society based upon equality

249. DEMARCATION – to set or mark boundaries

250. INQUISITION – a severe interrogation; a systematic questioning

251. AMELIORATE – to make better
     EXACERBATE – to make worse

252. CONTIGUOUS – sharing an edge or boundary; touching

253. DESICCATE – to thoroughly dry out; totally arid

254. PERTINENT – relevant and to the point

255. COMPLICITY – association or participation in a wrongful act

256. EXONERATE and EXCULPATE – to free from blame or guilt

257. INDISPUTABLE – not open to question; irrefutable

258. PRECEDENT – an action or decision that serves as an example

259. UNPRECEDENTED – without a previous example

260. MALFEASANCE – misconduct or wrongdoing by a public official

CHAPTER 8: WORDS WITH MULTIPLE MEANINGS

261. ARREST – to bring to a stop; halt

262. GRAVITY – a serious situation or problem

263. PRECIPITATE – a result or outcome of an action

264. RELIEF – elevation of a land surface

265. CHECK – to restrain; halt; contain

266. FLAG – to become weak; to lose interest

267. DISCRIMINATING – selective or refined taste

268. ECLIPSE – overshadow; surpass

269. COIN – to devise a new word or phrase

270. STOCK – a stereotypical or formulaic character

271. CURRENCY – general acceptance or use

272. BENT – a strong tendency; a leaning or inclination

273. COURT – to attempt to gain the favor or support of a person or group

274. NEGOTIATE – to successfully travel through, around or over an obstacle

275. TEMPER – to soften; moderate

276. PEDESTRIAN – undistinguished; ordinary; conventional

277. CAVALIER – an arrogant attitude

278. SANCTION – official approval/disapproval of an action

279. COMPROMISE – to reduce quality or value of something

280. CHANNEL – to direct along a desired course

CHAPTER 9: THE TOUGHEST WORDS – I

281. LAMBASTE – denounce; strongly criticize
282. QUIESCENT – inactive; very quiet
283. PROVISIONAL - temporary
284. LURID – sensational; shocking
285. TRUCULENT, PUGNACIOUS, BELLIGERENT
    – defiantly aggressive; eager to fight
286. PROPITIATE – to appease; conciliate
287. ÉLAN – great enthusiasm
288. PERFUNCTORY – performed in a mechanical, spiritless manner
289. APLOMB – admirable poise under pressure
290. OPACITY – impenetrably dense; hard to understand
291. CRAVEN - cowardly
292. VENAL – corrupt; open to bribery
293. LICENTIOUS and DISSOLUTE – immoral; debauched
294. NOXIOUS – harmful; injurious to physical, mental or moral health
295. SUPERFLUOUS and EXTRANEOUS – unnecessary; extra
296. DUPLICITOUS – deliberate deceptiveness
297. PROFLIGATE – very wasteful, especially of time and money
298. EPIPHANY – a sudden realization
299. INSIDIOUS – causing harm in a subtle or stealthy manner; devious

300. VACUOUS, INANE, VAPID – empty; lacking serious purpose

301. HARBINGER, PORTENT, PRESAGE – an omen that something will happen

302. BELEAGUER – to be beset with problems

303. BURGEON – to rapidly grow and expand

304. IMPERIOUS – domineering and arrogant

305. PETULANT – peevish; irritable

306. COMPLAISANT – agreeable; amiable

307. FAWN – to behave in a servile manner; subservient

308. OBDURATE, INTRANSIGENT, INTRACTABLE – very stubborn; unyielding

309. REDOLENT – exuding fragrance

310. CHICANERY – deception by artful subterfuge; deliberate trickery

311. CONUNDRUM – a difficult problem; a dilemma with no easy solution

312. SLIGHT – a disrespectful or disparaging remark; a put down

313. CAPITULATE – to surrender; to comply

314. DISHEARTENING – very discouraged

315. APOCRYPHAL – of questionable authenticity

316. MAGISTERIAL – learned and authoritative

317. PLASTICITY, MALLEABLE, PLIABLE – can be molded into any shape

318. CHAGRIN – feeling of distress caused by humiliation or embarrassment

319. OBSTREPEROUS – nosily and stubbornly defiant; boisterous

320. IDYLLIC – charmingly simple and carefree
321. DILAPIDATED – broken-down; in deplorable condition
322. EXTEMPORIZE and IMPROVISE – to speak without notes
323. MYRIAD – many; numerous
324. UNGAINLY – awkward; clumsy
325. DILATORY – habitually late; tardy
326. VITUPERATIVE – bitter criticism
327. DISCORDANT – a note of disharmony
328. PERFIDIOUS – treacherous; traitorous
329. PROLIFERATION – to rapidly increase
330. INDOMITABLE and RESOLUTE – very determined
331. MORIBUND – approaching death
332. NUANCE – a slight degree of difference
333. FLIPPANT and FACETIOUS – treating serious matters lightly
334. CREDULOUS – easily convinced; gullible
335. FLORID – very flowery; excessively ornate
336. EXCORIATING and SCATHING – expressing strong disapproval
337. INTERLOPER – an intruder; a gatecrasher
338. CEREBRAL – intellectual rather than emotional
    VISCERAL – instinctive rather than rational
339. NONPLUSSED and CONFOUNDED
    – completely puzzled
340. IGNOMINIOUS – disgraceful; shameful

CHAPTER 10: THE TOUGHEST WORDS –II

341. IDIOSYNCRASY – a trait or mannerism peculiar to an individual

342. CENSORIOUS and CAPTIOUS – highly critical

343. CONSTERNATION – a state of great dismay and confusion

344. DIDACTIC and EDIFY – intended to provide instruction

345. ELUCIDATE – to make clear or plain

346. EFFUSIVE – unrestrained praise

347. PROLIFIC – very productive

348. FUROR – a general commotion; an uproar

349. PARANOIA – irrational fear

350. MARGINAL and PERIPHERAL – of secondary importance; not central

351. OBFUSCATE – to deliberately confuse

352. FLUMMOX – to confuse; perplex

353. SPATE – a large number or amount

354. INEFFABLE – a feeling that cannot be put into words

355. HISTRIONIC and OVERWROUGHT – excessively dramatic

356. PLACATE – to soothe or calm

357. ESCHEW – to avoid

358. STOPGAP – a temporary solution

359. FLOTSAM – floating wreckage; debris

360. RESTITUTION – compensating for a loss

361. CHURLISH, SULLEN, SURLY – ill-tempered; rude

362. DISQUIETING – disturbing; upsetting

363. ORNATE – characterized by elaborate and expensive decorations; lavish

364. EXECRABLE, ODIOUS, REPUGNANT
    – detestable and repulsive

365. PERSPICACIOUS, PRESCIENT, DISCERNING
    – very insightful

366. ECLECTIC – using a variety of sources

367. HIATUS – an interruption in time or continuity; a break

368. VERTIGINOUS - dizziness

369. ESOTERIC and ARCANE – obscure information known by a few people

370. SUPERCILIOUS – haughty and arrogant

371. CUPIDITY – excessive greed

372. UNDERWRITE – to assume financial responsibility for a project

373. DISCOMFITED – to make uneasy; state of embarrassment

374. TACITURN – habitually quiet

375. SINECURE – a job that provides income but requires little work

376. LUGUBRIOUS – sad and mournful music

377. COSMOPOLITAN – worldly; sophisticated
    PROVINCIAL, PAROCHIAL, INSULAR
    – isolated from the mainstream

378. FECUND – intellectually productive or inventive

379. OSTENTATIOUS - showy
380. GUILE – treacherous cunning; skillful deceit
381. SANGUINE – cheerfully confident; optimistic
382. SCINTILLATING – sparkling; shining
383. PRISTINE – pure and uncorrupted
384. RAMPANT – unrestrained; unchecked
385. PERNICIOUS – highly injurious; destructive
386. OBLIVIOUS - unaware
387. REFRACTORY – obstinately resistant to authority or control
388. GARRULOUS, VERBOSE, LOQUACIOUS – very talkative
389. CONVIVIAL – fond of feasting, drinking and good company
390. BRUSQUE and CURT – abrupt; discourteously blunt
391. TEPID – lukewarm; mild
392. PROTEAN – taking on many shapes and forms
393. SOLICITOUS – showing great care; attentive
394. DISINGENUOUS – not candid; insincere
395. VENERATE and REVERE – to greatly respect
396. CONTENTIOUS – argumentative; disputatious
397. PRECLUDE – to make impossible; to rule out
398. COMPUNCTION, CONTRITION, REMORSE – sincere and deep regret
399. DEMOGRAPHY – the study of the characteristics of human populations
400. APHORISM and AXIOM – a statement universally excepted as true; a maxim

Index

Index

Index

Index

Index

Index

CPSIA information can be obtained at www.ICGtesting.com
235301LV00002B/56/P

9 780981 818467